Parents and Schools

Bright Ideas
Management Books

Published by Scholastic Publications Ltd,
Marlborough House, Holly Walk,
Leamington Spa, Warwickshire CV32 4LS

© 1988 Scholastic Publications Ltd

Written by Mike Sullivan
Edited by Jane Hammond
Sub-edited by Melissa Bellamy
Illustrations by Sue Lines

Printed and bound by Richard Clay Ltd,
Chichester.

ISBN 0 590 709401

Front and back cover: designed by Sue Limb

Contents

Introduction

'The no-man's land between home and school is a minefield strewn with explosive emotions and prejudices. In the increasingly difficult circumstances in which some are expected to teach and in the face of the often wild criticisms schools in general have to endure, it is not altogether surprising if some teachers feel, at times, reluctant to spend all the time and effort required to establish a close rapport with parents.'

Times Educational Supplement,
1 October 1982

In less than a decade there has been a tremendous change in the way that education in general, and primary education in particular, has been viewed by parents, teachers and politicians. The belief that education is the sole responsibility of the professionals no longer wins widespread support. While politicians and the media have created a climate of intense public concern over standards in schools, accountability and appraisal have become the catch-phrases of the day.

Yet against this backcloth of concern and suspicion there have been many areas of positive growth. Most schools have become more responsive to the community at large, both in informing the community of the work that goes on in classrooms, and in drawing from the expertise to be found beyond the school gates.

Recent legislation has attempted to give greater control of schools to parents, but partnership between parents and schools is not a matter of control and power. To be successful it must be based on trust and goodwill.

Establishing, maintaining and sustaining a good relationship between school and community is a time-consuming and demanding task. However, official guidance and identification of good practice in this area has been slow in coming. Both *Primary Education in England: — a Survey by HM Inspectors of Schools* (1978) and *Education 5—9: an Illustrative Survey on 80 First Schools in England* (1982) pay little attention to the contribution that parents can make to the formal education of their children. Indeed, the foreword of the 1978 report makes it clear that, at that time, they would not discuss the wider link between home and school, as their major concern was the work done in classrooms.

Consequently developments have been spontaneous and from the grass roots level. The purpose of this book is to pull together examples of ways in which schools can work with parents and others.

Chapter One

The school and the community

It is important that we project a positive image of schools to the community. Schools provide a public service, and so we should make some efforts to assure the community that their investment in the education system, and our school in particular, is worth while.

If we take and maintain the initiative then we are less likely to be ambushed or taken by surprise. We remain in control of situations, we can grasp opportunities as they arise, and we can anticipate trouble, avoid it, defuse it, or — if necessary — fight battles on chosen ground in our own time.

Many schools already invite parents to school events, such as exhibitions of

work, school plays, carol services and sports days. Other interested audiences from the community can be identified and invited to share in these activities. Local senior citizens clubs normally respond with enthusiasm to invitations to attend concerts, musical performances and sports days. Exhibitions of project work based on the local area will draw in a wide cross-section from the neighbourhood, although posters and perhaps a leaflet campaign, organised by willing parents, may be needed to gain maximum impact.

Once in the school, visitors' attention is usually directed at specific events and displays, but their interest will also turn to incidental features. New, perhaps more realistic, impressions of the school, the children, the staff and the sorts of work undertaken, may then be formed.

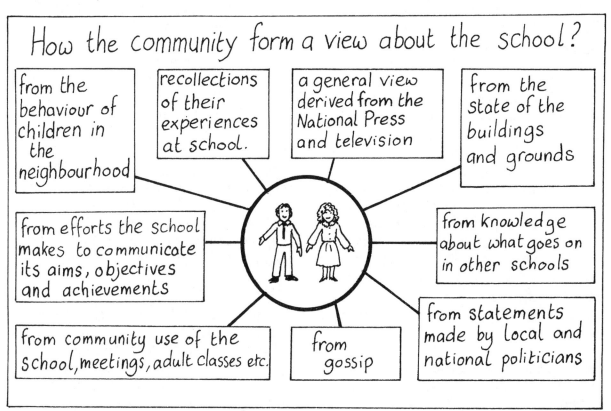

How the community form a view about the school?

- from the behaviour of children in the neighbourhood
- recollections of their experiences at school.
- a general view derived from the National Press and television
- from the state of the buildings and grounds
- from efforts the school makes to communicate its aims, objectives and achievements
- from knowledge about what goes on in other schools
- from community use of the school, meetings, adult classes etc.
- from gossip
- from statements made by local and national politicians

Community use of the school

The school buildings are major capital assets which belong to the community. In many areas schools are being designated as community schools, with a director and staff appointed to organise and administrate leisure and recreational activities, as well as the more traditional evening and holiday courses.

If, through falling rolls or a more flexible use of accommodation, space can be freed within the school for community use, this could well be an idea worth developing. Of course the school will lose surplus space, but it will gain through having more interesting and interested adults on the premises, providing opportunities to share resources and expertise.

Evening and weekend use
Outside normal school hours the Cubs, Brownies, Scouts and Guides could use the school hall and fields. This type of organisation caters for the children's leisure-time needs, and the activities frequently dovetail into the school's curriculum. Other clubs and organisations for children and young teenagers may also find the school an attractive and useful base. The community's evening centre could lay on evening classes for adults if there is enough local demand. Religious organisations could also make use of the school for teaching and for services.

The responsibility for teaching, supervision, administration and publicity would lie with the organisers of the activities.

Before making any commitment, it is essential to check with the relevant LEA department. The school caretaker will also need to be consulted about access to the buildings after normal school hours and any additional cleaning or tidying up that may be necessary.

Community activities during the day

If a classroom is free for part of the week, it could be used by an existing mums' and toddlers' group or a new one could be created.

The local social services department will provide advice on setting up and registering such a group, and may even provide an experienced worker on a temporary basis who can help to establish it.

Ideas for the community notice board

1) Register of childminders
2) Notice of school events
3) Meeting place and meeting times for :– mums + toddlers group. Toy library, scouts, cubs, guides, brownies etc.
4) Addresses + tel. no. of School governors, clinic etc.
5) Details of evening classes in the area
6) Details of community events – carnivals etc.
7) Items for sale/ exchange

Making school a welcoming place

First impressions are vitally important. As visitors step through the doors they begin to make judgements about the school, the staff and the children. A clutter of milk bottles, faded and badly mounted children's work, a lack of signs and directions, all convey clear messages about standards of care.

Schools are intimidating to many people. A welcome notice at the door, with the names of the headteacher and secretary, and perhaps a simple map, gives new visitors confidence and an immediate impression that the school is aware of and sensitive to the needs of others.

A display of named photographs of the staff, prominently placed in the entrance hall, can also be helpful to strangers to the school.

The staff of Elizabeth House Primary

Mrs. Eacher — Head Teacher | Mrs. Baker — Secretary | Mr. Smith — Deputy Head
Mrs. Jones | Miss Evans | Mr. Davies
Miss Smart | Mrs. Day | Mr. Brown — Caretaker

A fresh, attractive display of children's paintings and 3-D work in the entrance hall conveys messages to both children and adults that the work is valued, and that the school takes pride in sharing it with all visitors.

If milk crates must be kept near the main doors, store them in a low cupboard neatly concealed behind a curtain.

It isn't always possible for the headteacher to drop everything to see an unexpected visitor, but finding time to see parents must be a top priority. Some comfortable chairs arranged around a coffee table outside the office will help visitors to relax and take the strain out of waiting.

The visitor's impression will be more favourable if there is a range of booklets produced by children and some informative literature about the community and the school neatly displayed on the table. A small notice apologising for keeping visitors waiting and inviting them to look at the booklets adds the finishing touch.

Open all hours

If your school adopts a 'parents are welcome' policy, is it consistent to leave parents and children to huddle at the gate in unpleasant winter weather until the bell goes for school? Should parents, some with babies in push-chairs and prams, be instructed to wait outside the school doors until the children are sent out to them at the end of the school day?

The alternative is to encourage parents to come into school at these times, where they will have the opportunity to look at displays of their children's work. If their attention isn't attracted to the work on show in the corridors and entrance hall, look again at the standard and boldness of the displays. Once parents are in the corridor, they can be approached in an easy and natural way in those few moments just before and just after school to discuss informally aspects of their child's progress.

Prams, push-chairs and dogs ought to be left outside to keep the school clear of obstructions. Stagger the finishing times of classes slightly so that congestion in the corridors is reduced.

Have a word with parents if their conversations or behaviour are disturbing the children's work in classrooms, and insist on no smoking in school. They will appreciate your concern for the children's welfare.

Projection into the community

Although events held at the school may be well publicised, and invitations to visit the school persuasive and appealing, it may still be difficult to capture general interest.

To draw the maximum attention to the children's work, find a shop window in the high street to capture passing attention. Shopkeepers are reluctant to give prime window space, but building society offices are usually most generous with space and see an attractive display of children's models and paintings as part of the community service. Large supermarkets will sometimes provide space in their entrance areas, but work can quickly become damaged and soiled through the sheer volume of busy shoppers passing through. The local librarian will often enthusiastically agree to displays of children's work in the library.

It is vital that all work on public display is well mounted and neatly labelled, as it carries a number of messages about the school as well as the children. It shows that the school regards the children's work as important and expects it to be of interest to others. It reveals the sort of work undertaken and valued by the school, and the standards achieved.

A school float in the local carnival, exhibits in the children's section of the flower show, and entries by the school choir or groups of instrumentalists in the local music festival are all effective ways of creating a greater public awareness and pride in their school.

The school as a support service

Traditionally there have been strong links between parents and primary schools. Parents often tell teachers about family problems which are likely to effect their children. The problems are usually minor and temporary, in which case sympathetic understanding over a cup of coffee is all that is needed.

However, there are more serious family problems which a parent may bring to the school, such as the death of a parent, divorce, child abuse, long-term serious illness, a parent or child who has broken the law or has legal or financial problems. In these situations the school can and should put the family in contact with other 'caring services', such as social workers, the school's medical officer, educational welfare officers, or an educational psychologist.

It pays to develop close personal links with a named person in each of these services, and for the headteacher and at least one other senior member of staff to share knowledge of cases and contacts.

ELIZABETH HOUSE PRIMARY

How well do you know the local patch?
Some teachers in your school may have roots in the local community, and an extensive local knowledge. However, if your school is in an area with great mobility of population, the picture can be very different, with teachers having no previous links with the area in which they work and perhaps commuting to the school over a considerable distance.

Developing an effective and relevant curriculum depends partly on sensitivity to the local community, knowledge about its structure and the major issues and priorities within the neighbourhood. Positive steps should be taken to ensure that knowledge about the neighbourhood is based on fact rather than supposition.

Points for staff discussion could include the following:

1 What is the pattern of housing in the area and in what ways does this have a bearing on the upbringing of the children?

2 What is the main employment of parents?

3 What is the unemployment situation and how does it effect the children?

4 If there are minority ethnic groups in the community, what are the differences in their values and background? How does the school respond to these differences?

5 What is the main religious bias in the area?

6 What recreational facilities are available to the children and their families?

7 What potential does the community and the neighbourhood present for starting points in active learning?

8 In what ways can the school be developed as a source of positive growth within the community (eg sharing the use of the buildings and other facilities)?

Parents and children from ethnic minorities

At a time of increasing mobility of population there must be few schools that are not enriched at some stage by ethnic minority children.

Gathering detailed information about their language, religion and the culture of their homes, so that effective and sensitive links are created and maintained, can be an enormous task. In most urban areas, LEAs have established, well-organised multicultural and intercultural educational support services which offer information and practical assistance. 'Section 11' funding is usually available for extra staffing and resources.

However, in areas with small numbers of children from ethnic minorities, LEA specialist provision is thin or non-existent, and schools and families are left very much to their own devices.

Communications
1 What is the language spoken at home?
2 What knowledge do parents have of English?
3 Do families have problems with written communication from school? If so, is there anyone in the community who can offer and provide a voluntary translation service?

It may be necessary to translate all letters and notices.

Educational systems
1 What is the extent of parents' experience and knowledge of the British educational system?

2 Do parents and teachers share the same expectations about curriculum content, discipline and teaching methods?

Parents with little or no experience of the British educational system have to rely much more heavily on teachers for information about what goes on in school and the level of progress that their children are reaching relative to their peers.

Some points to consider in developing effective relationships with families from ethnic minorities

Religion and culture
1 What is the religion and culture of the home?
• How are the culture and background of the home reflected in the curriculum?
• Should the school make a collection of materials that reflects the home culture, including mother-tongue books?
• Can the school share in the celebration of non-Christian religious festivals?
2 Are there any special cultural or religious regulations that govern the children's dress or food? How does the school respond to these requirements?
• What about PE and swimming?
• What about the wearing of jewellery?

Advice and help
1 Is there an LEA adviser with
responsibility for multicultural work who
can offer help and advice?
2 Are there agencies in the local
community which can help?

Finding out the answers to these and
other questions is best done by going out
and talking to parents and others. Too
often we act on assumptions and
speculations bearing little relation to fact
or evidence. See pages 141-144 for a list
of helpful books and materials.

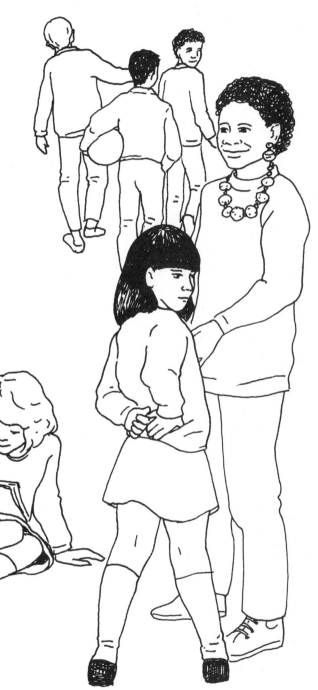

Chapter Two

Communicating with parents

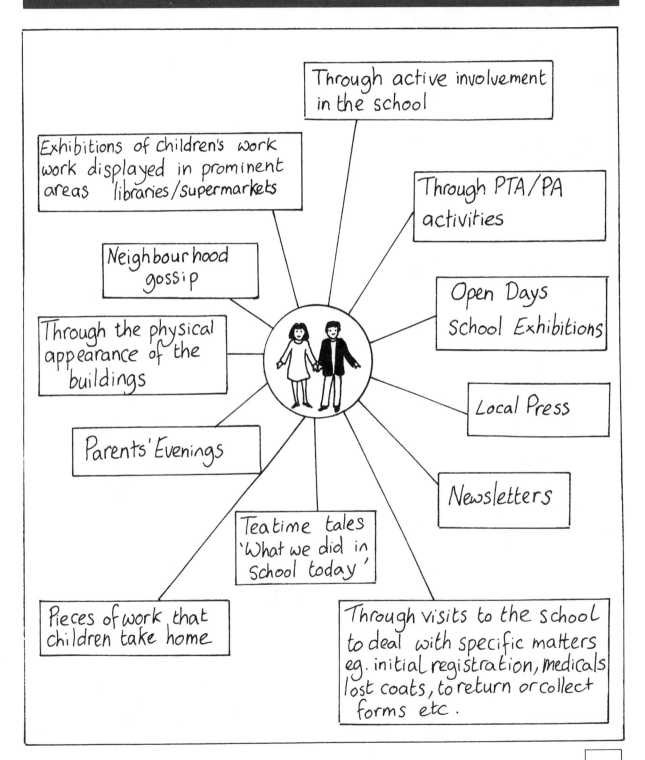

Through active involvement in the school

Exhibitions of children's work work displayed in prominent areas libraries/supermarkets

Through PTA/PA activities

Neighbourhood gossip

Open Days School Exhibitions

Through the physical appearance of the buildings

Local Press

Parents' Evenings

Newsletters

Teatime tales 'What we did in school today'

Pieces of work that children take home

Through visits to the school to deal with specific matters eg. initial registration, medicals lost coats, to return or collect forms etc.

Infant schools and departments can open up lines of communication with parents when the children are as young as six weeks. Simply ask the local health visitor to distribute leaflets to parents, offering congratulations, listing contact groups, and giving advice about registering for a place in the mums' and toddlers' group, nursery class, and full-time schooling.

The first meeting

It is difficult to imagine a situation much more intimidating for a parent than visiting a school for the first time, only to face a busy headteacher who brusquely demands responses to a very official-looking questionnaire.

However, helping parents to relax and feel at home isn't too difficult. 'Are you new to the area? Is your new house very different? Have you met the neighbours? I expect you'll find it handy for the shops/buses/school' are the types of comments which will make them feel more at ease.

New parents will bring their child with them and possibly younger brothers and sisters too. Keep a selection of toys in the headteacher's cupboard so that the children can play happily, leaving the adults to carry on an uninterrupted conversation. This shows the parents that you know and care about children, and shows the children that school is rather a nice place.

It's easy to overload a parent with too much information at the first meeting. Details of the address, telephone number, child's name and date of birth are perhaps all that need to be obtained at this stage. Give the parents an opportunity to ask questions and let them have some literature to take away to read at home.

You could make an appointment at this stage for the parents to visit again for a tour around the school, guided by another member of staff or, even better, a helper who lives near the newcomer.

Letters from school to home

Do the letters we write to parents ever reach home? If they do, are they ever read? It's too easy to blame a forgetful child and apathetic parents when lines of communication break down. Letters from school to home have to compete for attention with the constant bombardment of circulars, free newspapers and 'junk mail'. So it is hardly surprising that some school letters either fail to reach the parents or, at most, are briefly skimmed and immediately forgotten.

Therefore, to be effective, written communication from school to home must be readable, attractive and relevant.

Policy

Work out a policy for written communication with parents which is reviewed regularly. Points to consider might include distribution, reply slips, style and impact, and the review could involve some market research: write the same piece of information in a variety of styles and layouts and ask a group of parents to comment on the impact and effectiveness of each one.

A clear, well thought out policy will ensure that:
• important and urgent information is dealt with separately from routine, background material,
• by carefully checking on the distribution of important letters and recording the return of reply slips, there is a certainty that the message has been received,
• the needs of minorities are recognised and given appropriate attention,
• children appreciate the importance of passing on letters to parents; asking 'did you remember to give mummy or daddy the letter?' often creates an amazing improvement in the delivery rate,
• our use of language is direct and economical,
• our style of writing is friendly and personal,
• the communication is visually appealing through a sensitive use of layout and illustrations,
• we constantly check with parents on the effectiveness of our communications and ask them for suggestions for improvements; it is important to read letters from a parents' point of view,
• our newsletters are not just begging letters,
• the publication of letters has an even spread, both in content and frequency; three letters arriving in the same week asking for sponsor money, school photograph money and money for a school trip is unlikely to add to the stock of goodwill.

However, you may not want to go as far as one popular headteacher who ended school letters with 'Love, Flo'!

Watch your language!

Schools, as yet, are not part of the Civil Service, but letters from school can be as impersonal as any EEC analysis of pilchard packing in Portugal!

Rather than demonstrating our extensive vocabulary range and knowledge of educational jargon, we should be aiming for clear, direct and friendly communications.

Remember that most parents of primary school children are young, have very little spare cash and are in the early years of marriage. Letters can be informal and friendly without becoming patronising. 'I write to inform you . . .' can easily be replaced by the less stuffy 'a note to let you know . . .'.

Go for impact

All teachers have been conditioned to develop a 'waste not, want not' attitude. When faced with a blank sheet of paper and the task of writing a letter to parents, the great temptation is to fill the paper, and to squeeze in paragraphs covering a whole range of issues, so that the one important issue you want to deal with goes unnoticed and any impact is lost.

Letters should have a visual impact, too, which immediately captures the parent's attention and holds it until the message is absorbed.

Use a photocopier to incorporate children's illustrations to highlight your message.

With an ink duplicator you can cut out a simple frame stencil, with the school's name as a heading. Run off a large number of sheets and store them ready for future use. All the letters can then be typed within the limits of the frame and quickly run off. The result is a pleasing professional finish which is easily recognised.

Print each batch of letters on a different-coloured paper, so parents know that the crumpled ball of coloured paper at the bottom of the PE bag is a new letter from school which needs to be rescued and read.

Copies of news and other letters can be enlarged using the photocopier, and displayed in strategic places around the school to catch the parents' attention.

ELIZABETH HOUSE PRIMARY

Dear Mums and Dads,

Family Entertainments

On Thursday, 11th May, Gary Stardust and his puppets are presenting a performance of "The Sorcerer's Apprentice" at 7pm. ending at about 8.30pm. The show has had excellent reviews and is suitable for children of all ages. Tickets, priced 20p, are available from school.

PTA Fashion Show

High fashion at low prices comes to Elizabeth House on Wednesday 17th May, at 8pm. Most of the clothes are perfect though there are a few seconds. Admission 20p for adults, 10p children and OAP's.

Keep Fit

Ladies' "Keep Fit" classes start on Monday, 1st May at 8pm., admission 20p.

Yours sincerely,

T. Eacher.

Welcome and goodbye

The two letters below illustrate some of the points made about style and content. Copies of the first letter are addressed to the children about to be admitted to the reception class. Parents are already being encouraged to share reading with their children!

The second letter, which is sent to the parents of fourth-year leavers, neatly brings to an end a chapter in a relationship.

ELIZABETH HOUSE PRIMARY

Dear

I am pleased that you are starting in Mrs Allsopp's class on -- September. You will have lots of fun with Mrs Allsopp and learn all sorts of interesting things.

You will soon make a reading book and also learn to do some writing.

Mummy or Daddy will bring you to Mrs Allsopp's classroom at 9 o'clock and will fetch you home at 12 o'clock or 3 o'clock. They will want to know all about the things you have done.

Mummy or Daddy will need to get you a pair of plimsolls and shorts or a leotard for wearing in the hall.

You will go swimming on Thursday at 9 o'clock.

Have a nice holiday. I am looking forward to seeing you in September.

Mrs Watts

ELIZABETH HOUSE PRIMARY

Dear

We are now rapidly approaching the end of the school year and we are feeling rather sad as we prepare to say goodbye to our fourth-year children. Most of these boys and girls have been with us for nine years, and in that time I hope we have built up a happy relationship with them and yourselves.

Although it makes us sad, it is good for the children to move on. The time has come for them to make a start with new friends, new teachers, new subjects and new surroundings. We hope that they do well and we look forward to hearing about their successes.

It is sadder still when the last child in a family leaves and the link between the family and Elizabeth House is broken. To those parents, the staff and I send our thanks for the co-operation we have experienced over the years and for the generous response we have received to all our appeals.

Yours sincerely

Mrs L Watts

Distribution

What happens to notes and newsletters for the parents of children absent from school? Copies could be marked with the child's name and pinned to a specially reserved area of the class notice-board or kept in the class register until the child returns.

Giving another child a spare copy to put through the absent child's door is an unreliable and unsatisfactory solution.

WANTED

MUMS & DADS

To attend a 'Maths Evening' at Elizabeth House on Tuesday, 20th November at 6.30p.m.

Do come and find out about our new maths scheme! Children will be demonstrating the scheme in action and our new computer.

- - - Please Return the Slip Below - - -

I/We would very much like to attend the 'Maths Evening' at Elizabeth House on Tuesday 20th November.

Signed _____

Reply and acknowledgement slips

Some messages are quite important but still do not justify being sent through the post. Acknowledgement or reply slips are a useful way of establishing that papers have safely arrived home and have been read to the end.

Chasing up reply slips is time-consuming and not always totally successful, but the parents who don't return slips can be identified easily, and alternative means used to ensure that they 'get the message'.

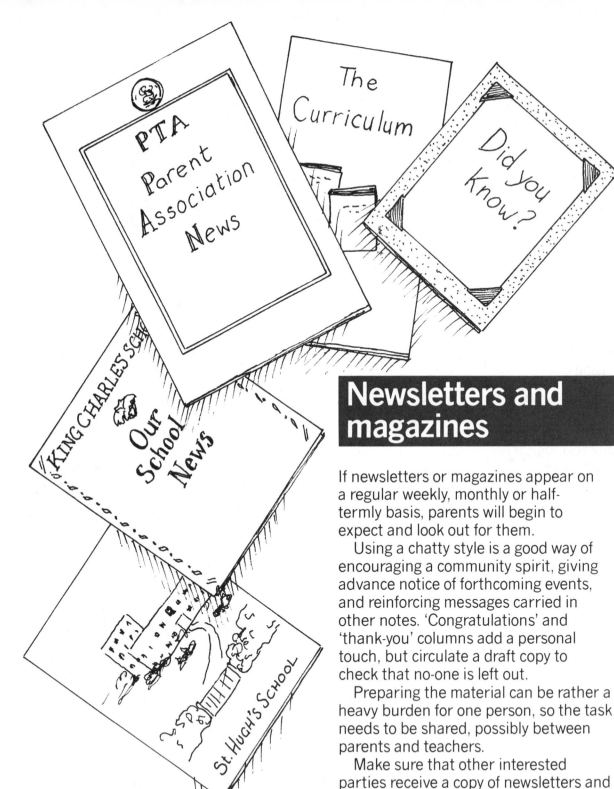

Newsletters and magazines

If newsletters or magazines appear on a regular weekly, monthly or half-termly basis, parents will begin to expect and look out for them.

Using a chatty style is a good way of encouraging a community spirit, giving advance notice of forthcoming events, and reinforcing messages carried in other notes. 'Congratulations' and 'thank-you' columns add a personal touch, but circulate a draft copy to check that no-one is left out.

Preparing the material can be rather a heavy burden for one person, so the task needs to be shared, possibly between parents and teachers.

Make sure that other interested parties receive a copy of newsletters and magazines, such as the caretaker, the cleaners, the cook and the school crossing patrol.

A selection of headings for a monthly or half-termly magazine

Did you know?
A general 'chit-chat' about recent events and around school: visits, visitors, exhibitions, competitions etc.

The curriculum
Projects to be undertaken in the coming weeks; requests for relevant information and the loan of materials; invitations to curriculum meetings and workshops.

Happy birthday
Individual greetings to children.

PTA/parents' association news
A chance for the group's secretary to write about social, educational and fund-raising events.

Thank you
An important part of any magazine: parents are more likely to offer help if appreciation of their support is shown when things are going well.

Welcome to school
A welcome to individual children and families which have recently moved into the area.
You may also want to mention those children who have left the school.

In profile
General profiles of new staff, existing staff and those who are leaving, help to create a more personal and friendly atmosphere. Caretaking, ancillary and kitchen staff should also feature regularly in this section.

Congratulations
Births, marriages and successes of past pupils all provide interest and add to a sense of community.

Forthcoming events
Advance publicity for forthcoming attractions at the school.
This section can also be used to highlight events taking place in the community which deserve the school's support.

Sports activities
Successes and failures of the school's teams, achievements in the British Amateur Gymnastics Award, awards gained during the school's swimming sessions, and so on.

Written reports on children's progress

The subject of written reports for parents is one which frequently arouses controversy in staffrooms.

Most staff feel a responsibility towards parents and believe that they should give an account of children's progress at least once a year. At one time, the written report provided the principal link between school and home. Children were tested and graded, and a summary of results with a set of brief comments dispatched to parents.

This style of report has generally fallen into disuse because:
• parents tended to focus attention on the child's place in the class league table rather than on the acquisition of skills and concepts,
• modern approaches to the primary school curriculum emphasise the importance of self-motivation and the intrinsic value of learning rather than overt competition,
• while giving an outward appearance of objectivity, tests and testing in primary schools were shown to be idiosyncratic, subjective and unfair,
• comments were necessarily brief and without a frame of reference, and could often be misinterpreted.

ELIZABETH HOUSE PRIMARY

Report on ....
.... Term ....
Class .... Class Position ....
No. in Class ....

Arithmetic (Mental and Problems) ....
Reading ....
Composition ....
Dictation ....
Handwriting ....
Spelling ....
Art ....
Music ....
Games ....
....
General Comment ....
....

Class Teacher ....

With the adoption of more open approaches to parents and the introduction of regular parents' evenings, the value of written reports has diminished. Before parents' evenings, teachers reflect on the progress of individual children and make notes. In many schools these notes are tidied up, written out on a loosely structured report form and given to parents after a face-to-face discussion.

Interest Areas School studies	Keenly interested Comment	Developing interest	Not yet interested
Music			
Art			
Craft			
P.E.			
Games			
Swimming			
Test Results: General comments			

Name . . . .   Class Teacher . . . .

This report is based on the child's work during the school year 198_

Standard of work   Good Average Weak   Effort Good Average Weak

(compared with children in the same group
Basic subject & skills (Please enter comments where appropriate)

	Good Progress	Show Improvement	Needs to Improve	Stage in scheme
Reading				
Comprehension				
Written English				
Oral Work				
Spelling				
Handwriting				
Mathematics				

The report letter

Instead of using a standard report form, some schools send parents individual letters outlining their child's strengths and weaknesses. Although this is more time-consuming for the teacher, it provides the opportunity to be selective in the styles of language used, so that effective communication can be made without using clichés.

However, although written reports can be useful reminders to parents of their children's progress at school, they are no substitute for direct contact between parents and teachers.

Talking with parents

Writing to parents is of secondary importance compared to oral communication. It is the face-to-face contact with parents which can make or break a good relationship.

Parents deserve respect and attention. They may not know too much about the merits of alternative approaches to the curriculum and various forms of organisation, but they do know when people are being insincere, glib and patronising. They know when their views and opinions are not given due consideration or treated seriously.

Address the parents by name whenever possible to emphasise that they are important to you.

Many of the situations in which face-to-face contact with parents occurs are dealt with in later chapters.

Booklets, handbooks or brochures

Under the 1980 Education Act, LEAs are responsible for providing information to parents about individual schools. This information, in most cases, is presented in a straightforward, factual but rather bland way. What is often missing is any flavour of individuality or character.

To supplement the official document, many schools produce a prospectus in the form of a booklet, handbook or brochure. With careful planning and editing this will provide parents with a handy source of reference for all sorts of practical information and advice, written in a more chatty style.

Your local teachers' library, resources centre or college of higher education may have a collection of school handbooks for you to browse through.

The School Prospectus Planning Kit, published by the Advisory Centre for Education, contains a great deal of useful information and examples drawn from a range of schools.

It is essential to ask parents, teachers and governors for their views before going into print. You will want the final product to be polished so that, with enough forethought and planning, it will not need to be reviewed for some time.

Items to include in a handbook
- School aims: the broad aims and objectives of the school.
- School hours: starting time, finishing times and the importance of punctuality.
- School organisation: grouping, single age classes, mixed ability and provision for special needs.
- Absence and health: what to do when a child is absent; illnesses common in childhood; symptoms and periods of infection.
- School meals: arrangements for the collection of money; free meals; special provision.
- Parents' visits to school: just dropping in; appointments and parents' evenings.
- Special clothing: uniform, PE clothing, painting overalls, jewellery and valuables in school.
- Arrangements for swimming: who goes and when; costumes and swimming hats.
- School fund: purpose and arrangements for collection; the school tuck shop.
- Parents' association: organisation and typical activities.
- Governors: organisation, purpose and meetings.

Details which can change fairly frequently, such as staff, governors and school holidays, can be included in a separate annual supplement, so that the booklet, handbook or brochure doesn't become dated.

To present information in an attractive way, use a triple-folded sheet of A4.

Below is yet another way of organising a triple fold.

One of the problems with a school handbook is that it often ends up at the bottom of the kitchen drawer, never to be found when needed. With enough funds you can avoid this by combining the handbook with a school year calendar.

The illustration shows a layout which is both attractive and useful — just the thing for the kitchen wall. Keep the size within the limits of A3 and use good quality card. A commercial printing firm was used for this calendar to obtain a professional finish, and the project was funded by the school's parents' association.

As the calendar is produced annually, school holiday dates and the names of staff and governors can be included.

Parents unable to read English

There may well be some parents unable to read English. They may be from another country or, as in the case of some traveller families, have never been to school.

If so, you will need to make special provision to ensure that all these families receive the same standard and quality of information as the others.

Normally parents in this situation have learned to cope and will not welcome separate attention, but if problems occur, the situation needs to be handled with sensitivity, tact and imagination. If your school serves a traveller community on a temporary or semi-permanent basis, and there are problems over written communication, contact your regional traveller education service for help and advice.

English as a second language

Many LEAs have produced booklets in a number of languages to enable parents whose mother tongue is not English to develop a greater awareness and understanding of what goes on in schools. The school's adviser/inspector may be able to provide copies of materials written in a variety of languages such as Bengali, Cantonese, Punjabi and Urdu.

In areas where there are concentrated groups of people whose first language is not English, there is usually a detached service of advisory teachers to provide schools with help, guidance and support. However, in areas where there is a scattered distribution of ethnic minority families, support for schools is patchy or even non-existent, and both schools and parents are left to muddle through.

These parents may be almost totally unfamiliar with our education system, and will need explanations about organisation, routines and curriculum. The value of aesthetic and physical education and learning through play may well have a different status in the educational system of their countries of origin.

If the school doesn't bother to gather appropriate information, and neglects the task of effectively communicating with parents from ethnic minorities, confusion and misunderstandings will inevitably occur. A list of useful books and other resources can be found on pages 141-144.

Chapter Three

Parents and the curriculum

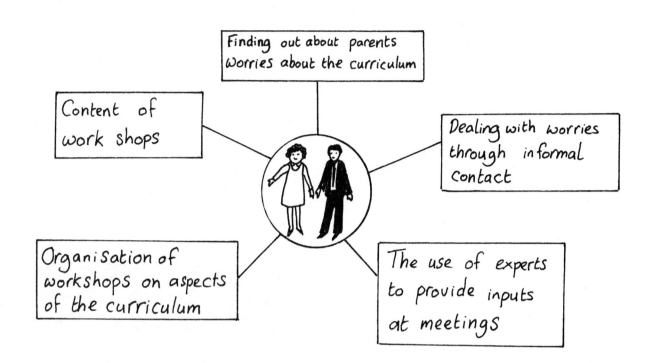

It is important to discover, preferably at the first meeting between parents and school, the sorts of expectations the parents hold, and to match these against the framework of experiences and activities the child will encounter at your school. Parents will often measure the success of the school by the way it meets, or fails to meet, these expectations.

Ask about the sorts of tasks their child can already do, and the sorts of tasks they will expect the child to do after the end of the first year. Talk about what the children in the relevant age range can achieve, and begin to discuss ways in which parents and school can share in developing learning.

When children move on to new schools they will be enthusiastic and excited, but also perhaps a little apprehensive.

Therefore it also makes good sense to hold a meeting for both parents and children to discuss with headteachers and members of staff the transfer arrangements and the ways in which continuity will be maintained. Parents should be reassured that, although there will be new opportunities and challenges, previous learning will be built upon and not neglected. Also take this opportunity to let parents know about all the records that will be transferred with their children.

Dealing with parents' worries

The report *Improving Primary Schools,* chaired by Norman Thomas for ILEA, identified the following as common worries of parents: pace of learning, insufficient memorisation of arithmetic tables, the teaching of spelling and grammar and puzzlement about schools' approach to mathematics. The report stressed that there is an urgent need to reduce any unnecessary worries which may arise from misunderstanding or ignorance.

Make sure the headteacher and staff are around the corridors and classrooms at the beginning and end of the school day to give parents and teachers the opportunity for purposeful conversation. Useful information can be exchanged both ways which would not justify a special meeting. Such opportunist and informal meetings are exceptionally valuable, and need to be exploited to the full, but there still needs to be a systematic approach to the exchange of information between parents and teachers to avoid misconceptions being generated or sustained.

A whole range of approaches are needed to give a balanced view of the functions and aims of the school. Apart from open days, exhibitions of work, parents' evenings, newsletters and occasional booklets about the curriculum, workshops are a particularly valuable way of informing parents about the structure of the curriculum — why we carry out certain tasks and the order in which they occur.

However, providing parents with information about the curriculum isn't enough. They also need to know about the ways in which we motivate children through praise and reward, and the teaching strategies we employ as we implement the curriculum.

Practical activity or an opportunity to work alongside a group of children draws an enthusiastic response and valuable discussion is generated. These practical activities must provide some insight into the sorts of learning the children are engaged in. A greater understanding usually leads to a greater appreciation of the work of the school but, at the end of the day, if we fail to convince the parents of the effectiveness of our approach then perhaps we are not really convinced ourselves.

One school's experience

What follows is an example of how one primary school tackled the task of informing parents about the introduction of a commercial maths scheme. Purpose and planning are vital, so some detail is given about the preliminary discussions and decision-making.

Once the staff had decided to introduce the new scheme, the headteacher and some of the staff members discussed the issues with the school governors at one of their regular meetings and showed them the materials. As there was some suspicion that the scheme might involve 'new maths' with little traditional arithmetic, an impromptu workshop took place there and then. The merits of the scheme were quickly recognised and the governors' endorsement readily obtained.

The headteacher and staff soon realised that if the governors were anxious about changes in the maths curriculum, then parents would probably share their concern. They felt that parents should be made aware of the new maths scheme and have an opportunity to see it in operation as soon as possible.

An item in the newsletter towards the end of the summer term informed parents of the staff's excitement at the introduction of the scheme. It was to be introduced throughout the school in the autumn term. Many staff meetings were held in the summer term for the teachers to familiarise themselves with the materials, organise the resources and decide how the work was to be matched to the children.

Within weeks of starting the scheme, both children and staff felt confident enough to organise a session for parents.

A preliminary letter was sent out asking parents whether they would welcome an opportunity to learn more about the scheme and about 70 per cent expressed interest.

Sample groups from each class were invited into school one evening. They were arranged in the main hall to carry on with some work supervised by their teacher, and parents were invited to observe the work and tackle some assignments themselves. As there were only small groups of children, the teacher had some freedom to discuss specific points with parents; also by having everyone in the same room, the headteacher was able to give a general introduction to the sorts of maths experiences the children encounter at school, and the ways in which parents can help their children to learn about maths.

Getting the whole show together!
* Plan it well!
* Leave time for questions
* Leave time for discussion
* Don't start with main points, there may be latecomers
* Refreshments — when, where, how, what?

Preparation

All members of staff were made to understand clearly the purpose of the meeting and the part they were expected to play.

Coffee, tea and biscuits were arranged, giving a natural opportunity for informal discussion. (Parents don't normally mind paying for refreshments on these occasions.) Examples of children's work were displayed, including photographs of children working at tasks associated with the workshop.

Handouts were prepared for parents to take away, so that they could refer back to the notes to clarify their thoughts in a more relaxed atmosphere at home. As always, plain language is vital. (If you begin with a presentation, don't distribute handouts too early, or the audience will read them instead of listening to you.) Handouts might include details of the scheme of work and record systems that are to be used, information about other publications that might be of interest to parents (particularly those which are available on loan from the school), and an invitation to come back for further discussion on any of the issues raised.

If there is to be some practical work, make sure that there is enough equipment and that it works; blunt scissors and floppy compasses say a lot about resource management!

Presentation

Don't spend all the time talking at parents, but keep the presentation brisk, business-like and to the point, always in terms of 'your children' rather than 'the school'. Most of all, make it interesting.

If the school possesses or can borrow a video camera, record the children at work and play it back to the parents. It's amazing how quickly children adjust to a video camera being in the classroom; after a short period of intense interest — and performance — it will be almost totally ignored.

A tape-slide sequence showing the children working can also be very effective.

The overhead projector is a valuable tool for presenting information in a visual form, although one of the pitfalls is that you can easily end up talking to the screen instead of your audience.

Keep it active

A variety of approaches and groupings were used to keep up the momentum of the workshop.

It is far easier for people to express an opinion or to ask questions in small

Stimulation

zzzz   zzzz

* Make it interesting!
* If you have nothing new to say, well why are you saying it?

* Talking to the overhead projector may end up with it being your only listener.

group settings, and it is important that everyone has a chance to make a contribution. Address people by name and make sure that members of the groups get to know each other. Keep the groups balanced and intervene politely if one or two hog the discussion, using your management skills to give less self-assured parents the confidence to contribute.

Bringing the session to a close

At the end of a session all the groups were pulled together, the purpose of the session restated and feedback obtained, followed by a summing-up. Ideas for future events were given an airing, and profuse thanks offered to parents and helpers for their time and support.

The visiting expert

It is often a great temptation to invite a specialist to talk to parents about a particular aspect of the curriculum. The result is usually a confident and entertaining lecture, sometimes supported by some practical activities.

But parents are interested in the specific learning experiences their children will encounter in the classroom, and the real experts in this area are the school's staff.

There is a role for the 'expert' in providing advice, guidance and encouragement, giving support from a back-seat position.

The local primary school adviser will be able either to provide practical support, or to put the school in touch with other schools where good practice is taking place.

Performance!

* Entertainment value has some importance — BUT content is the priority!

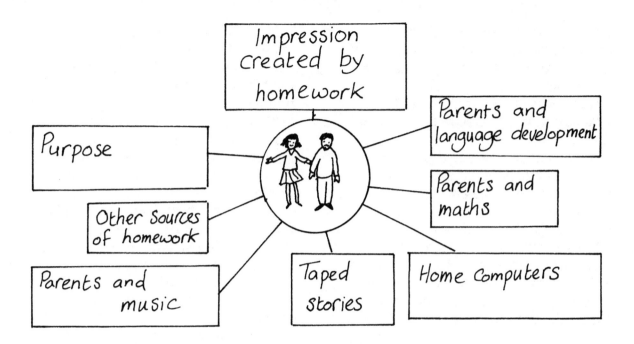

The diagram shows a central circle (with two figures) connected to boxes:
- Impression created by homework
- Parents and language development
- Parents and maths
- Home computers
- Taped stories
- Parents and music
- Other sources of homework
- Purpose

Homework

Homework is one way in which parents gain a perspective on the curriculum and become actively involved in their children's learning.

Too often the school bag contains little more than 'the spelling list', 'the reading book', and 'tables for the tables test'. Even if your school sets no homework at all, nearly all schools hold fund-raising activities which reinforce the 3Rs stereotype. 'The sponsored spell', 'the sponsored tables test', and even worse, 'the sponsored silence' all convey images of an elementary school at the turn of the century.

If our vision of the primary curriculum involves more than the 3Rs, shouldn't the tasks children undertake away from school reflect this vision?

Purpose

It is important to have a clear idea as to the purpose of homework.

There is little point in just sending books home. Parents need to be aware of the role they are expected to play.

However, the children should have sufficient skills, knowledge and motivation to complete the task with the minimum of adult intervention. After all, homework should be for children, not parents!

Improving Primary Schools identifies three advantages to be gained from giving primary children homework:

1 Children are made aware of the priority given by parents and teachers to the acquisition of skills.

2 The parents involved will know for certain that teachers give high priority to those skills.

3 Children have the benefit of more individual attention than the teacher can provide.

The report also stresses that special steps should be taken to make sure that children do not lose out if their parents are unable to help.

The Government White Paper *Better Schools* sets out the following as possible objectives for homework:

• to encourage pupils to develop the practice of independent study;
• to develop perseverance and self-discipline;
• to allow practice, where it is needed, of skills learned in the classroom;
• to permit more ground to be covered and more rapid progress to be made;
• to enable classwork to concentrate on those activities requiring the teacher's presence;
• to open up areas of study and make possible the use of material and resources of information that are not available in the classroom;
• to involve parents (and other adults) in pupils' work.

Activities outside school

Some children show special talent and interest in drama, music or sport. These children may be catered for by after school activities and clubs. However, sometimes the school can draw attention to associations, groups and organisations which are not directly linked to the school but can offer specialist coaching and facilities.

There are times when this kind of 'homework' can interfere with school work; some children, even at the age of ten or eleven, belong to a number of football teams in a variety of leagues and end up playing more football in a week than a professional!

If pressure on children becomes excessive, a meeting between someone from the school and the parents should be an urgent priority.

It is easy to forget, too, that children and families have lives which function independently of school, and that children can be engaged in a variety of educational, cultural and religious activities that impinge upon their free time. For instance, it is very common for Moslem children to attend classes on religion after school. Many children have music lessons and also need time to practise their instruments.

Unless the school is aware of and sensitive to these additional demands upon children's time, it could be making a child's life extremely difficult by imposing an extra burden of sometimes rather trivial homework.

Parents and language development

Research by Gordon Wells and others on oral language development has shown that those rich and extended conversations which provide the greatest learning opportunities take place between parent and child during shared activities around the home.

Once parents have gained a greater knowledge of the school and the sorts of learning experiences taking place there, further opportunities arise for conversation, reinforcing and extending classwork.

The shared activities can include reading, sorting out shopping and following up project and topic work.

Ideas for language development activities at home

• 'Simon says'
Touch your toes, hold your nose,
Touch your hair, sit on a chair.
    Don't forget to take it in turns to give the orders!

• 'I spy'
Use letter sounds before letter names. Extend the game to 'I spy something that ends with . . . .'.

• 'Sort the shopping bag'
Sort the shopping bag into piles of bottles, tins, boxes, frozen food, fresh fruit and vegetables.

• 'Sorting colours'
'Pass me the blue box. What's in that red bottle?'

• 'Naming items'
'Pass me the cabbage. Can you guess what's in this tin?'

• 'Making comparisons'
Compare large and small, heavy and light, hard and soft, tall and short.

Parents and mathematics

Encouraging and developing parental involvement in maths education has always been more difficult than gaining support for involvement with reading. Parents still doubt that work with sets, Venn diagrams and modulo arithmetic is more important than the rote learning of multiplication tables and the constant repetition of sums.

    Therefore, it is important to let parents know, through workshops, special maths meetings, parents' meetings, informal

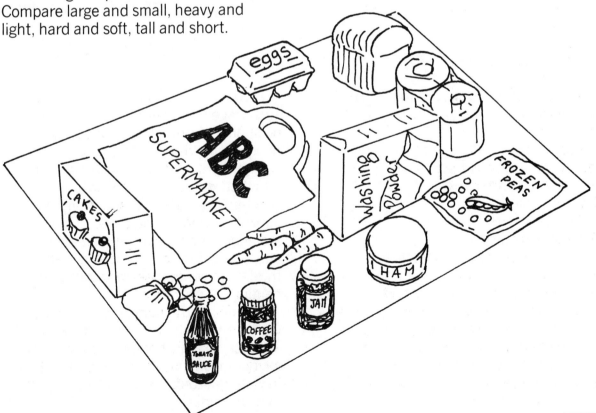

HELPING YOUR CHILD LEARN ABOUT MATHS

IDEAS CARD 8

FLOUR

reparation

250gm

HELPING YOUR CHILD LEARN ABOUT MATHS

IDEAS CARD 5

MONEY AND CHANGE

Let your child sort out the coins in your purse. How many brown coins? How many silver coins? What do we call one of these? What will I need to buy ..... ?

contacts and booklets, that the school's scheme of work includes the following:
• counting,
• measuring to make comparisons,
• measuring quantities,
• graph work (drawing and interpretation),
• practical work,
• telling the time,
• fractions (including decimals),
• shape,
• measuring angles and turning,
• activities involving addition, subtraction, multiplication and division.

Parents also need information about the sorts of activity they can undertake at home to develop their children's experience of mathematical ideas.

The language of maths can also be encouraged and developed at home: position (in front, behind, under, beside, beneath, up, down, on top, bottom left, bottom right); comparison (more than, less than, the same as, taller than, shorter than, lighter than, heavier than, equal to); shape (triangle, square, circle, rectangle, cube, cone); number (zero, one, two, three etc); order (first, second, third etc); money (coin recognition and naming).

There is also a wide range of games which, although not designed specifically as teaching aids, provide a great deal of incidental and enjoyable learning. These include dot-to-dot, snakes and ladders, and dominoes.

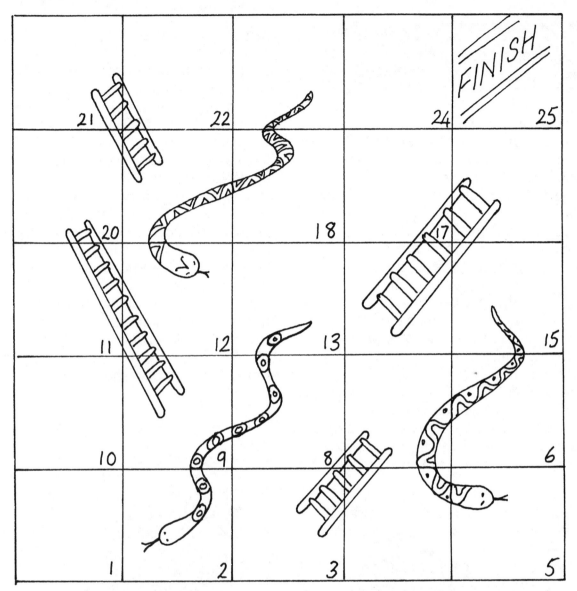

A SIMPLIFIED SNAKES AND LADDERS BOARD SERVES AS A USEFUL MEANS OF REINFORCING NUMBER RECOGNITION, COUNTING-ON AND ADDITION.

All games using two dice give practice of addition.

Putting the missing numbers on the board is also a useful and demanding exercise.

Parents and computers

If a child is lucky enough to have access to a computer at home, a great deal of worthwhile creative learning can be developed with a little time and expertise. Computer games are fun, but one problem is that children tend to develop the impression that the computer is in control of situations rather than a tool to be controlled.

Organise a 'computer evening', supported by an expert from the advisory service explaining the potential of computers as learning tools, linked with a column in the school's newsletter for computer news and contact information.

Setting up a computer club for children and interested parents is fairly easy, particularly if parents who already have some expertise can be roped in to help. Some of the school's computer equipment, particularly printers and turtles, can be harnessed to software which has been produced at home.

Most machines are capable of running a variant of the LOGO language which, compared with other computer languages, is quickly learned and straightforward to use.

It should be fairly easy to acquire a second-hand model of one of the more popular home computers, such as the Spectrum or Commodore 64, at knock-down prices. These make ideal machines for a computer club.

There is a large number of books on the market containing simple programs, including *Exploring Maths With Your Micro — a Book for Kids Aged 9 to 90* by David Johnson, published by Heinemann.

Parents and reading

In the past teachers have been rather cautious about involving parents in their children's reading. There were fears that they might not use appropriate methods, perhaps emphasising 'sounding out' with letter names rather than a more usual phonic or 'whole word' approach, or that they might push their children too hard and undo the good work done by the school on reading readiness and children's attitude to reading.

There was concern that only middle-class parents would enthusiastically co-operate, so that inequality of opportunity would increase. There were anxieties that if books were taken home they would be chewed by the dog or the baby and never be seen again.

Last, but not least, there was a feeling that the teaching of reading was a highly skilled task best left to the professionals.

However, a key factor in reading development is adult attention. The more time a child spends on reading and book-related activities with a caring, interested and interesting adult, the greater the rate of progress.

The obvious way to increase child-adult contact time for reading activities is to encourage parents to take on more responsibility in this area.

Through working together, parents and teachers should develop a greater understanding of what each contributes to the child's learning. By being exposed to a wider range of children's literature parents will develop a deeper insight into what reading is about and the pleasure that can be gained from it.

In the last eight years or so a whole range of reading schemes encouraging parental involvement have been developed. There are three distinct approaches, and a whole range of variations on these themes.

Whatever technique parents are encouraged to adopt, the emphasis needs to be on enjoyment and satisfaction. The home should be a place of pleasure and relaxation and not just an extension of school.

Parent listening

If the parent listening approach is taken, the process of beginning to read is explained at parents' meetings first of all, together with ways in which parents can help children to master these techniques. The importance of the 'reading card' to monitor progress is stressed, and parents are often invited to write comments, so entering into a dialogue on progress with the teacher. Usually booklets are provided so that parents can refer back to these as the project progresses.

An example of this approach is given by Griffiths and Hamilton through their work in Hackney with PACT (Parents, Children and Teachers). Other examples are the Bellfield Project in Rochdale and the Haringey Project, both of which have been reported extensively; some details can be found in Bloom's *Partnership with Parents in Reading* (Hodder & Stoughton). It has been claimed that this approach results in twice the normal rate of progress.

Paired reading

Usually in paired reading the parent reads a passage of a book to their child, then the parent and the child read the same passage together with the parent providing the error words. Sometimes parents are encouraged to fade out their contributions as the child gains confidence but joining in again if the child encounters difficulties. A useful book on paired reading is *Parental Involvement in Children's Reading* by Keith Topping and Sheila Wolfendale (Croom Helm).

Prepared reading
This technique involves the parent and child talking about the book before the reading session starts. The conversation can include a summary of the book so far, trying to guess what happens next or simply a discussion about the illustrations. The parent then reads from the book, the child silently reads the same piece and then reads aloud with prompting from the parent when needed.

What should children read at home?
Reading is more than the mastery of complex mechanical skills; it is a gateway to a whole variety of knowledge and experiences. Parents should encourage children to devour the printed word in whatever form it appears. Comics, magazines, football programmes, recipes, instruction sheets and books from the local library are just as important as the books in the reading scheme.

One advantage of the reading card is that parents can enter details of their child's informal reading activities: 'Jane didn't read her book last night because she was reading her new computer magazine' should be a matter for celebration rather than censure.

Taped stories
Parents and teachers can work together

to produce a library of taped stories which children can listen to at school and at home. Keep the tape and the original story book together in a clearly labelled transparent bag, so that cataloguing and the running of a loan service are simplified. The ten-minute cassettes sold for computer programming are cheap, normally of a high quality and long enough for younger readers.

It is worth investing in a few commercially produced stories on tape so that techniques of pace, presentation and page cueing can be studied.

The local library
Parents and children should be encouraged to visit their local library regularly to make use of the facilities. Children's librarians are usually eager to respond to invitations to visit schools, to display work produced by the children, to talk to children at school and to lay on holiday activities at the library.

Parents and music

Children often begin to play a musical instrument at primary school but, without the opportunity or encouragement to practise at home, progress is slow and enthusiasm drops away.

The school could produce a booklet about learning to play an instrument which gives guidance to parents and children. If the school has no music specialist, ask the LEA music adviser for help.

You could even lay down a condition that, if a child is to borrow an instrument belonging to the school or is to receive specialist tuition, parents must sign a 'contract', promising to insist on regular practice and to fill in a daily practice record.

Parents and topic work

Parents can be a tremendous source of materials and information for topic work. With encouragement and the promise that materials will be well looked after, parents will often allow all sorts of interesting family treasures to be brought to school — perhaps an old gas mask, grandad's war medals, a flat iron or old photographs.

Parents may agree to come in and talk about their work or the local neighbourhood some years ago. They will need to be reassured that the event will be as painless as possible and hopefully even enjoyable! Sometimes parents and other visitors are happier talking to a small group of children who then report back to a larger group.

More ideas for useful homework

The following ideas for homework assignments are taken from the Schools Council Working Paper 75 *Primary Practice: a Sequel to the Practical Curriculum* (Methuen). They have been most successful with eight- to eleven-year-olds.

• Look for patterns on wrappings, wallpaper and curtains in connection with some mathematical work on tessellations.

• Identify and classify different materials in the home to study their properties in subsequent science lessons.

• Record the cost of certain grocery items to compare the cost per unit weight.

• Find the location of local police stations, hospitals and fire stations to find later on a map of the area.

• Measure the perimeters of rooms in the house, following work on linear measurement.

• Find labels and containers marked in imperial and metric measurements, to add to the class conversion graph.

• Monitor the family's intake of food for a day, following a television programme or other work on health and diet.

• Interview parents about their jobs after a discussion about the life of a newspaper reporter.

• Write an identikit description of a parent to use in group work concerned with the differences between people.

• Make papier mâché masks or objects using a balloon as a base, following a preliminary effort at school.
• Collect different types of lettering from magazines and newspapers to develop various formats for work on illuminated lettering.
• Write a percussion accompaniment to a tune composed at school and written out by the teacher.

The parents' bookshelf

A bookshelf or bookcase could be devoted to books and booklets on the curriculum for parents to borrow. Include books describing ways in which parents can help at home (see 'Useful publications' on page 141), and copies of workbooks and other materials used by the children (not necessarily to use at home, but to help parents understand what their children are talking about).

Inviting parents into the classroom

An open invitation to all the parents to visit school and see their children at work is a recipe for disaster, risking a large number of parents turning up together.

A personal invitation to two or three parents at a time, gradually working through all the parents in the class, is a much more effective approach.

It is a great advantage to have a second member of staff in the classroom at the same time to cope with the routine class management tasks. This frees the class teacher to talk to the parents about the work taking place, the way in which the children are grouped and the materials used.

Coping with criticism

Genuine partnership is a two-way process. If the school tells the parents how to help their children to learn at home, the parents are likely to reciprocate with advice about how to improve the provision made for their children in school.

How do teachers in your school react when their professional judgement is challenged by a parent? Is a parent who asks difficult questions regarded as a difficult parent? Are there some parents and members of staff who seem to gain satisfaction from stirring up trouble for others? Does the school have ways of redirecting their attention to activities where they will cause the minimum of damage to relationships between school and parents?

Through close links with parents and a fair amount of parental involvement in school, it is usually possible to anticipate matters of discontent or controversy, and to take the heat out of situations before they boil over.

This knack of spotting potential problems and skilfully side-stepping them is useful, but there are times when teachers need to dig their heels in and confront issues. For instance, you may discover that particular parents are using inappropriate methods in bringing up their children. They might neglect their children, or have unrealistic expectations of them, making them miserable in the pursuit of unreasonable goals. Some parents are grossly over-indulgent, while others are unreasonable in the demands they make on the teachers and the school.

Beyond the sensible limits of 'give and take', the school must take a firm stand. Winning the support of parents shouldn't necessitate total appeasement and abandoning professional judgement. The school's authority resides in knowledge and experience.

Conversely, there are bound to be parents who are unimpressed by what the school has to offer. The school's perspective on what it can and should do for an individual child may be very different from the parents' view. If disagreements are profound and fundamental, and once all avenues of compromise and flexibility have been explored, it may be in the best interests of the child to seek a transfer to another school, where curriculum, organisation and ethos more closely match the parents' vision.

Chapter Four

Special events

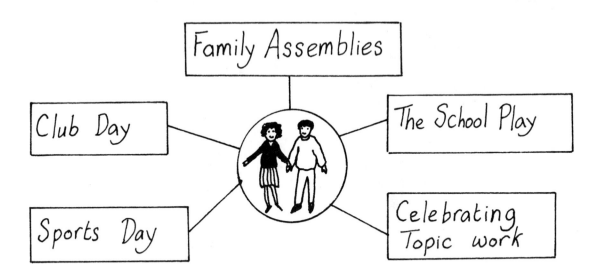

Family Assemblies

Club Day

The School Play

Sports Day

Celebrating Topic work

Family assemblies

It is quite common for schools to hold family assemblies on a regular basis where a group of children and their teacher take on responsibility for the service.

Parents need as much notice as possible so that they can make arrangements to attend. Send out a list of dates and classes early in the term, followed up by individual written invitations from the children to their parents as the date for their personal contribution approaches.

After the assembly there is another opportunity for the headteacher and other members of staff to meet with the parents and informally discuss matters of interest.

The school play

The school production can be a tremendous way to use the talents of children and staff, incorporating the values and skills held dear by the school. It is an opportunity to draw together music, movement, drama and art, and to share these with an appreciative and supportive audience. Parents will also be able to see the care that is taken in making the school an attractive environment, and evidence of the quality of relationships between teachers and children.

Parents and grandparents are particularly interested in what their children or grandchildren are doing and will turn out in even the worst of weather to see them perform. So, to attract a

ELIZABETH HOUSE PRIMARY PRESENTS

ROBIN HOOD

FRI
16
DEC
7.30

15p

Robin Hood Cast
* * * *
Narrator — Donna Broadway
Robin Hood — Tyra Chadburnd
Maid Marion — Lisa Gunter
Sheriff of
Nottingham — Simon Lowbridge
Little John — Colin Weeson
Curt Jester — Claire Lolley
Bella — Lee Webber
Scott Dingley
Michael Davies
Lorraine Bradford
Mille
Mark Spener
Richard
Elizabeth Lee Evan
* * *

large audience, the cast list will need to be large.

An illustrated programme listing the entire cast could be photocopied and distributed. Attractive programmes are often retained as treasured mementoes of school days.

Parents may want to bring cameras to record their offspring's finest moment, but taking flash photographs during a performance is distracting and annoying. Announce before the start of the performance that there will be an opportunity for photographs after the final curtain. Alternatively, invite parents to take photographs at the dress rehearsal.

Parents' help can often be invaluable in making costumes and props, and in the dressing-room before and during the performance. Also, with parents' help,

the children could lay on simple refreshments for the interval.

It is important that in the excitement invitations to governors and other friends in the community are not forgotten. The local newspaper may welcome an invitation to send a photographer along to the final rehearsal.

Senior citizens particularly welcome invitations to the final dress rehearsal, especially if nursery or very young infants are involved in the performance.

Celebrating topic work

At worst, topic work fizzles out as interest dwindles, half-completed models become recycled junk, and folders of work taper out in unfinished sentences.

To avoid this, build up to an exhibition or display of writing, artwork and models, to which parents and friends are invited (not the kind which requires visitors to weave their way through a labyrinth of corrugated cardboard, feeling neither excited nor stimulated by what they have seen). With a little extra imagination and effort at the planning stage of a project, particularly a whole-school project, it is quite easy to direct the work to a spectacular and worthwhile climax for children and parents.

Outlined below are four examples of projects which have been developed in this way.

Pets and other animals

One of the most popular tasks for a group of children to undertake is a project on 'Pets and other animals'. A tremendous amount of valuable work can be developed from this topic, including graphs, classifying, weighing, measuring and observing. Children are very keen to bring in pets from home and both parents and children often have and are willing to share expertise.

A grand finale which naturally suggests itself is a pet show. A local vet or RSPCA officer may be willing to act as judge. One of the first tasks will be to send letters home, containing an entry form. The animals need to be divided into four groups: dogs, cats, birds, and other creatures.

Set a maximum number of entries — about 25 animals can be judged in a half-hour session. It is essential that dogs are brought on a suitable collar and lead, and that no bitches in season are entered! If the dogs are judged first, the prize-winners can be kept in school for the final parade and parents can take the rest of the dogs home.

Prizes could be awarded for:
• the dog with the coldest nose,
• the best looked-after dog (evidence of vaccination can be taken into account),
• the dog whose tail wags most,
• the dog with the friendliest eyes.

Cats will need to be brought into school in a suitable box or basket. Prizes can be awarded for:
• the best looked-after cat,
• the cat with the longest whiskers.

The birds will need a quiet area. Present prizes for:
• the bird with the brightest plumage,
• the best looked-after bird,
• the bird with the prettiest song.

The 'other animals' may well range from mice to ponies, so give some thought to where large animals can be tethered outside the building. If the pet show is run in the autumn or winter, ban the entry of hibernating animals. In the 'other animals' category, prizes can be awarded for:
• the most unusual pet,
• the best looked-after pet.

As a last word of advice, if you are tempted to run a school 'pet show', make sure the caretaker is available with a mop, bucket and pan, although pupils and parents are usually careful to look after and control their pets, and everyone thoroughly enjoys the day.

Magic and mystery

A project on 'Magic and mystery' shouldn't be an exercise in frightening children but needs to include lots of 'good magic' and 'happy endings'.

There are lots of fine traditional stories and numerous recent children's fiction books, such as *The Worst Witch*, by Jill Murphy, and Hamish Hamilton's *Book of*

Magicians, edited by Roger Lancelyn Green, which will provide good starting points. There is enormous scope for written work, art and craft, and science, and maths can be linked to the project through work on magic squares.

End the project with a fancy dress competition, with prizes for the best-dressed witch and wizard, and entertainment by a professional magician. Refreshments could be packaged and labelled with suitable descriptions.

Display children's work on the theme in the school hall and corridors, so that children can show their parents their own personal contribution.

Circuses and fairs

A project on 'Circuses and fairs' contains tremendous scope for work across the curriculum. Children will have fun in PE and games lessons developing a few of the skills of circus entertainers. For example, three-ball juggling can be mastered by junior children, while walking on empty coffee tins leads to low stilt-walking.

The excitement generated during this project can be shared in an entertainment laid on for parents at the end of the project. Decorate the school hall to look like a circus ring and get the children to put on a variety of circus acts.

The Normans and the Middle Ages

Work on 'The Normans and the Middle Ages' can be brought to a close with an adapted mummers' play with knights in cardboard armour, dragons, jesters and minstrels. The school hall would need to be transformed into a castle banqueting hall, and refreshments laid on so that parents eat a simple cold buffet as they

are being entertained.

Again, corridors could be crowded with examples of children's writing, pictures and models based on the project.

Sports day

Sports days are great fun for parents and children. Make sure there is a range of light-hearted competitions and that all

the children have a chance to take part in a number of events. A high proportion of novelty events not only maintains spectator interest, but also increases the opportunities for less athletic children to win.

Public address systems are usually unreliable and need to be backed up by a printed programme of events. (Designing a cover for the programme can be yet another competition.)

Parents need advance notice if there are to be parents' races. However, it is important that they aren't pushed into taking part in events against their better judgement. Not only could they lose face in front of their children, but sudden and excessive strain on those who are not physically fit can be dangerous.

Parents may be tempted to leave at the completion of the events in which their children have taken part. To prevent this sort of exodus, events for different age groups need to be mixed in the programme.

Finally, it is particularly important that young children do not feel they have failed if they do not win their event. It is easy to print off certificates for all children taking part, and even contrive situations so that everyone receives a prize.

A club day

One way to arouse awareness of organised activities for children in your area is to invite local organisations to make contributions to a club day. Clubs, associations, play group organisers and the local children's librarian can all be invited to take part.

Displays of posters, photographs, equipment and membership details need to be assembled and representatives of the organisations invited to give talks and presentations. Parents appreciate invitations to these talks, so plan the day carefully and draw up a timetable of activities. Those children who already belong to any of the organisations should be given a chance to talk about it from their point of view.

Active recruitment on the day should be discouraged, although it does make sense for children to take home leaflets describing the sorts of activities available.

If the event is held early in the autumn term, staff of local further education institutions may welcome an opportunity to display details of courses for adults.

Chapter Five

Parents outside the curriculum

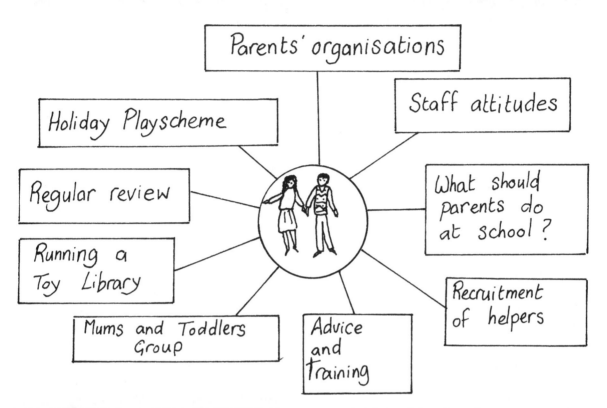

Parents' organisations

Staff attitudes

Holiday Playscheme

What should parents do at school?

Regular review

Running a Toy Library

Recruitment of helpers

Mums and Toddlers Group

Advice and Training

Parent-helpers in school

Some parents will be willing and able to offer the school unpaid assistance for a few hours a week on a regular basis. There will always be needles to be threaded, cookery tasks to be supervised, swimmers to be dried, pots to be washed and readers to be heard.

The parents can gain a great deal of satisfaction from helping the school, the children will benefit from the extra adult attention, and teachers will be delighted to have all those time-consuming, sorting and tidying jobs done by someone else. But there are pitfalls: without clear planning and consultation, difficult situations can arise, sometimes resulting in confusion and bad feelings.

Staff attitudes
Are all the staff convinced that it is a good idea to have parents helping around the school? Their continual presence in school may be seen as a threat, as if they are constantly checking up on teachers' activities and gathering gossip for the school gate.

The secretary and ancillary staff may feel their jobs being threatened and their professionalism and skills being eroded as unpaid parents undertake their work.

Staff should be encouraged to discuss their reservations and fears openly so that these can be allayed as far as possible. It is also important to arrange visits to schools where parental involvement is successful, so that staff can talk to teachers, non-teaching staff and parents about the advantages and disadvantages of this sort of support.

One problem which often causes friction is where parent-helpers should go during break-times. If they are invited into the staffroom, some teachers may feel that this is an intrusion into their privacy, and that they cannot relax in case they make an unguarded remark about a child, a situation or a colleague which could be misinterpreted and reported elsewhere. Perhaps a room could be set aside for parents, or the class teacher and head (or deputy) could take their break with the parents in the classroom.

Areas of involvement

It is essential that the ground rules of involvement are clear to everyone.

Should parent-helpers teach? Obviously parents would not be put in charge of a class for a day, but talking about their work or hobby to a group of children, or showing them how to make a cake or a model boat, could be seen as teaching. Perhaps they should only be asked to instruct children under the supervision of a teacher. This supervision would, of course, be indirect if the parent is working with children in another area of the school.

If they listen to children read, should they work with poor readers? Would we expect them to analyse the children's difficulties and give appropriate help, or is that the task of the teacher? How will the child who is a poor reader and the child's parents react to an unqualified neighbour becoming aware of the situation?

If parents help with sports activities outside school, other parents should be informed about the arrangements for supervision and asked for permission for their children to take part. The school must ensure that standards of supervision and coaching are appropriate for the age of the children, and that the parent helper is suited to the activity.

Transporting teams to away fixtures is a headache which can be eased by parents. Again, it is wise to obtain parental permission and to check that the parent providing transport is adequately insured.

Parents' help may also be needed for class or group outings, not necessarily to instruct, but perhaps to work on the maintenance of equipment and the preparation of materials.

A group of parents may well be interested in running a school bookshop, assisted by older children. A small stock of popular titles, ordered through a children's book club, can be displayed on a book stand, alongside second-hand books and an 'exchange book and comic' department. The second-hand stock is likely to be renewed through donations from parents as their children's tastes develop.

There are numerous DIY tasks that parents can undertake around the school. Carpentry jobs such as building cupboards and putting up additional shelving, painting home corner furniture, and making curtains and drapes, all help to brighten up the environment.

Parents can also run a regular rota to video programmes for school. They could take the tapes from a bank at school, record the programmes at home, and then return them for use in classrooms.

Recruiting parent-helpers
The staff could draw up a list of parents who they feel would be suitable, and then approach these parents on an individual basis. However, there are dangers that only a narrow social and ethnic band will be recruited, causing resentment among other parents.

Alternatively, all parents could be invited to volunteer, and a register of helpers kept with ways in which they can help. If this approach is used, a rota can be established and additional parent skills discovered.

Some parents may be considered unsuitable to work with large groups of children. Their offer of help should then be tactfully declined or, better still, they should be encouraged to help in activities which don't involve direct access to children.

At least one LEA has developed procedures for checking the possible criminal backgrounds of employees who have 'substantial access' to children. This is a very sensible precaution as, unfortunately, there have been rare incidents where helpers in schools have sexually abused children. It is impossible for a school to check on the background of parent-helpers, but the community 'grape-vine' tends to be particularly effective in alerting schools to potential problems in this area.

Advice and training
The headteacher should spend some time with each parent-helper, talking about the sorts of help they can give and the basic need for tact, diplomacy and confidentiality.

If parents are to help with reading, they should receive instruction about prompts, primes, praise and discussion.

Parents who provide assistance with art and craft activities need to know how to prepare, use and store materials. It is too easy for an over-helpful parent to bang in all the nails on a model whilst the children look on, or to make the cake mix and put it into the oven, untouched by children's hands. 'Showing how' instead of 'doing for' children doesn't always come naturally. Parents who are to help with practical activities need some simple guidance about what they are expected to do. A finished product of quality is important, but even more important is the quality of learning experience gained by the children during its production.

Helpers in the nursery and reception classes need to understand the value of play and how to bring about learning situations from play activities.

Some schools organise rather formal sessions and even award a certificate on completion of the training. Tutors could be a mixture of teachers, nursery nurses and experienced parent-helpers.

Other schools approach the matter in a much lower key — conversation over a cup of coffee between teacher and parent-helper is gently steered to cover the same topics.

Liability
If there is to be regular involvement of parent-helpers in the school, either the school or the parents' association should consider taking out insurance protection for those parents through the NCPTA or an insurance broker.

Mums and toddlers

A 'mums and toddlers' group within a school can serve a variety of purposes. It breaks down the feeling of isolation experienced by so many mothers with young children, enabling them to share knowledge and experience about childcare. It also gives the children an opportunity to play alongside others of the same age, and positive relationships with the school staff are established.

Efficient organisation and clear leadership are essential. Agreement must be reached about the purpose of the group and the activities to be undertaken.

The best mums and toddlers groups are more than 'gossip shops', with the children left to their own devices to play together in the corner. Activities are

organised for the children, and ways in which parents can help with their children's learning are explained, explored and developed. One activity the group could undertake is establishing and running a toy library.

Children learn a great deal through constructive play, so the provision of appropriate toys and other materials will encourage the development of a whole range of skills.

You could ask the National Toy Library Association for advice and guidance, but you will basically need a wide selection of toys, an area where they can be displayed, so that children can choose and try them out, and a band of volunteers to issue, collect, check and record loans.

Local charities and the parents' association may help with the initial purchase of materials. As all parents and teachers know, it is difficult to find inexpensive toys which are attractive to children and also have learning value. A small charge could be made for each loan, so that funds are gathered for additional materials, and to replace toys that become worn out or damaged.

Summer holiday play schemes

Why not instigate a holiday play scheme to be run by parents for all or part of the summer holiday? Don't forget to inform the school caretaker so that the school is open at the appropriate time.

It is best to have only one, and certainly no more than four, clearly indentified scheme leaders, who will provide a focal point for information and decision-making.

At an early stage, discuss the age range of the children who will take part and whether children who don't attend the school should be involved. Dates, times of sessions and charges must be agreed and well publicised before the end of the summer term.

You will need equipment for a variety of outdoor games, and paint, crayons, pencils and paper for indoor activities on rainy days. Include visits to the local swimming baths and park, and even more ambitious excursions to the seaside, for instance.

The parents in charge will need to have access to first aid equipment and the telephone, so that emergency services can be contacted if necessary.

Regular reviews

If you use parent-helpers in your school, it is important to review the situation regularly at staff meetings. Also remember to ask the parents for their views on how the system could be improved, and to thank them for their help.

Chapter Six

Parents' organisations

Many schools manage without any formal organisation of parents, or parents and teachers, but simply call on individuals or groups of parents to form *ad hoc* working parties for specific tasks. Fund-raising may be planned or organised by school staff, with parents roped in to support on the day.

In this situation, power rests firmly with the headteacher and staff; they set the agenda, determine the level of involvement, and control the outcomes. But this ignores or underestimates the abilities and creative energies of the parents.

However, at the other end of the spectrum, formal associations are in danger of falling under the control of strident, vocal minorities. Therefore it is best to build safeguards into the initial constitution of the association to constrain possible excesses without over-restricting initiatives.

There are a variety of organisational forms which can be used to channel parental support. These include PTAs, parents' associations and friends of the school. The titles reveal the sort of relationship between parents and teachers with which the teachers, at least, feel reasonably comfortable.

Setting up an organisation

It would be foolish to ignore the potential problems in setting up a formal organisation of parents within the school. There are those who seem to thrive on stirring up discontent and trouble, others who are wildly enthusiastic but grossly incompetent, and some who have particular bees in their bonnets. There may be problems with the management of funds, and there is always a number of parents who are too busy or apathetic to become involved in any organisation.

On the other hand, children need the active support of their parents if they are to derive the maximum benefit from their school, and elected governors need the opportunity to consult parents in an informal setting. Both parents and teachers need to develop trust and confidence in each other, and the task of raising money for those essential extras becomes easier if it is shared.

The following procedure for setting up a parents' organisation is recommended by the National Confederation of Parent-Teacher Associations.

An inaugural meeting
Write a letter (preferably addressed personally) to all parents, inviting them to an inaugural meeting.

Invite a speaker from the NCPTA (or the area federation, if there is one) to outline the advantages of a home-school association for children, parents and teachers.

Consult the headteacher about a suitable chairman for the first meeting, and arrange refreshments for the end of the evening to enable everyone to mix informally.

Then prepare the agenda and perhaps some suggestions for future events.

A sample agenda
1   Chairman's welcome.
2   Speaker outlines aims and activities of home-school association.
3   Resolution: that this meeting is in favour of forming a home-school association.
4   Election of committee: care must be taken to select a committee that represents all areas of the school community.
5   Date of first annual general meeting to consider and ratify a constitution.
6   Decision to affiliate to the National Confederation of Parent-Teacher Associations (which includes membership of the local area federation, if there is one).
7   Suggestions for possible future activities.
The committee should:

• prepare a constitution for the first annual general meeting to consider, amend and ratify. This can be held at any time within a year of the inaugural meeting;
• complete an application for NCPTA membership;
• arrange a programme for the year.

Model constitution
Please note that this is a model constitution. It may be varied to suit particular circumstances in each association. However, it is important to note clauses 2, 24 and 25. The wording of these clauses has been agreed with the Charity Commission and the Inland Revenue so that inclusion in their

entirety establishes an association as a charity for tax purposes.

1   The name of the Association shall be

....

2   The object of the Association is to advance the education of the pupils in the school; in furtherance of this object the Association may:

a   develop more extended relationships between the staff, parents and others associated with the school;

b   engage in activities which support the school and advance the education of the pupils attending it;

c   provide and assist in the provision of facilities for education at the school (not normally provided by the education authority).

3   The Association shall be non-party political and non-sectarian.

4   The Association shall take out public liability and personal accident insurance to cover its meetings, activities, officers and committee (note 1).

5   The Association may appoint a President.

6   The names of the Vice Presidents shall be submitted at the Annual General Meeting. (These are usually people the Association wishes to honour.)

7   Membership shall consist of all parents and/or guardians of pupils attending the school, and all teachers (note 2).

8   The management of the Association shall be vested in a Committee consisting of the following Officers: Chairman, Vice Chairman, Honorary Secretary, Honorary Treasurer together with . . . other members (note 3).

9   The Officers and Committee shall be elected at the Annual General Meeting and shall serve until the commencement of the next Annual General Meeting.

10   . . . members of the Committee shall constitute a quorum, (note 4).

11   The Committee may appoint subcommittees as it deems necessary, and shall prescribe their function provided that all acts and proceedings of any such sub committee shall be reported to the Committee as soon as possible, and provided further that no such subcommittee shall expend funds of the Association otherwise than in a budget agreed by the Committee.

13   Committee meetings shall be held at least once each term.

14   The Annual General Meeting will be held on . . . (note 5). At the Annual General Meeting, the chair shall be taken by the Chairman or, in his/her absence, the Vice Chairman of the Committee.

15   Nominations shall be proposed and seconded by members and shall have the consent of the nominee. Nominations may be made at any time prior to the commencement of the Annual General Meeting.

16   The Committee may fill casual vacancies by co-option until the next Annual General Meeting.

17   Auditors who are not members of the Committee shall be elected annually at the Annual General Meeting to audit the accounts and books of the Association.

18   Special General Meetings may be called at the written request of a minimum of ten members.

19   Thirty days' notice shall be given of any Special General Meeting to all members of the Association.

20   The Honorary Treasurer shall be responsible for keeping account of all income and expenditure and shall present a financial report to all committee meetings, and shall present the accounts duly audited for approval by

the members at the Annual General Meeting.

21 Bank accounts shall be operated in the name of the Association, and withdrawals shall be made on signature of any two Officers of the Association.

22 The financial year shall commence . . . (note 6).

23 Any matter not provided for in the Constitution and concerning the organisation and activities of the Association shall be dealt with by the Committee whose decision shall be final.

24 No alteration of this Constitution may be made except at the Annual General Meeting or at a Special General Meeting called for this purpose. No amendments or alterations shall be made without the prior written permission of the Charity Commission to clauses 2, 24 and 25, and no alteration shall be made which could cause the Association to cease to be a charity in law.

Alterations to the Constitution shall receive the assent of two-thirds of the members present voting at an Annual General Meeting or Special General Meeting.

25 The Association may be dissolved by a resolution presented at a General Meeting called for this purpose. The resolution must have the assent of two-thirds of those present and voting. Such resolution may give instructions for the disposal of any assets remaining after satisfying any outstanding debts and liabilities. These assets shall not be distributed among the members of the Association but will be given to the school for the benefit of the children of the school or, in the event of a school closure, to the school to which the majority of children of the closing school will go, in any matter which is exclusively charitable in law. If effect cannot be given to this provision, then the assets can be given to some other charitable purpose.

Notes

1 Membership of the National Confederation of Parent-Teacher Associations automatically provides this.

2 Membership can also include past parents, grandparents, friends of the school, ancillary staff and governors.

3 The size of the Committee should depend upon the number of children on roll. A small school might have a Committee of five plus the Officers, whereas a large school might have 12 plus the Officers. The headteacher may be a member of the Committee.

4 A quorum would depend on the size of the whole committee; it must be a third of the members (minimum three).

5 The Annual General Meeting should preferably take place during the autumn term to enable new parents to be involved from the start of the school year.

6 The financial year will be for 12 months.

The above approach may seem rather 'over the top', but a clear statement of aims and an agreement on the structure of the association enables a whole morass of potential misunderstanding, confusion and dispute to be avoided.

Some headteachers are even more cautious, incorporating into their constitution a 'headteacher's right to veto' and a 'headteacher's right to dissolve the association'.

Chapter Seven

Parents as governors

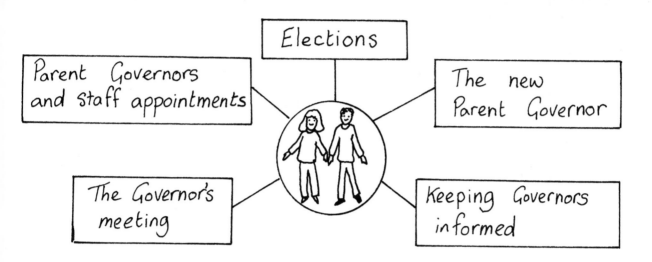

Elections

Parent Governors and staff appointments

The new Parent Governor

The Governor's meeting

Keeping Governors informed

At the time of Plowden and Midwinter in the mid-sixties and early seventies, the emphasis was on the school bringing a strong influence to bear on the parents and the home environment through the power of teacher expertise.

However, recent legislation has swung completely counter to this notion, attempting to put the parent in the 'expert' position, with influence and control over many aspects of school organisation and management.

One way in which the balance of power has shifted is through the development of individual governing bodies for all schools and increasing parental representation.

The governors, in theory at least, have control over planning and direction, but the headteacher has operational control over the running of the school, the head and staff being accountable for their professional conduct to the governing body. The governors also recommend the appointment and, in some cases, the dismissal of staff. In fact, governors are potentially a powerful influence in all aspects of school life.

In many staffrooms, there was initial suspicion and unease over the appointment of governing bodies to individual schools. Were they a threat to teachers' professionalism and autonomy, or just a minor irrelevance, merely 'rubber stamping' the headteachers' decisions?

The reality is rather different from these fears. There has been a steady growth in understanding of the value of governors as a sounding board for ideas providing access to opinion-makers in the local community, and as a pressure group to mobilise support and exact influence through channels not normally available to the school.

Joan Sallis, in *The Effective School Governor*, wrote about the parent governor who was advised that they had not been appointed as a parent representative, but as a representative parent. There may be times when the parent governor legitimately acts as an 'ombudsman' or 'shop steward', bringing parents' grievances to the notice of the headteacher, but in nearly all cases it is best if individual parents deal directly with the school.

The government of the school rests with the governing body as a whole, and not with individual members. The power base of governors is their collective advice, guidance and direction rather than personal opinion and independent action.

The governing body is made up of nominees of the education committee, teachers, parents and co-opted members. The appointment of co-opted members and education nominees is not the direct business of the school, whereas the election of teacher and parent governors is managed at school level. The election of teachers to serve as governors is usually a straightforward process, but the election of parent governors is more complex.

Election of parent governors

A survey of LEA arrangements for the election of parent governors carried out by the Advisory Centre for Education (ACE) in 1985, showed that there was a wide variation in advice given to schools. The ACE has, with the help of the National Association of Governors and Managers, produced a framework for guidance on election procedures for parent governors.

There was concern that many parents knew little of the duties and responsibilities of governors, and it was suggested that a two-part publicity campaign should be instituted, the first part informing parents about the role and functions of governors, and the second giving them details of the election dates and procedures.

Letters to parents, advertisements in the press, information leaflets on the role of parent governors, and even phone-in programmes on local radio were suggested as ways of creating interest.

It was also proposed that, as local authorities already staff departments to run local government elections, they could take much of the administration away from the school. If LEAs didn't react positively to this suggestion, a range of procedures was suggested which schools could use to make elections for parent governors as democratic and fair as possible.

Official nomination forms were recommended, on which parents could nominate themselves or someone else, with the nominee signing the form as an acceptance of the nomination. Candidates should also have the opportunity to provide a statement, no longer than one side of A4, to be distributed with voting papers.

It was suggested that voting papers should be carefully distributed to all parents, and returned to school between five and ten days later, and that voting should never take place exclusively at an election meeting. The candidates and a friend should be invited to attend the count, and candidates should have the opportunity to request recounts if this seems reasonable.

Results should be posted on school notice-boards, and parents should receive written notification of the results and the number of votes cast for each candidate.

One of the difficulties not covered by the report is that parents may be very reluctant to stand for election, even when they are fully aware of the importance of the post. When general exhortations fail, a certain amount of personal encouragement may be necessary. Of course heads and teachers should not attempt to subvert the democratic process, but asking, 'Do you know anyone who might serve?' is often all that is needed to bring about the nomination of a candidate who may have been rather hesitant to stand.

It is easy for vociferous minorities with unrepresentative causes to dominate parental activities, so try to encourage parents representing a broad range of views to stand for election.

If there are parents who are unable to read English, election materials must be produced in other languages. This should be the responsibility of the LEA rather than the school, particularly when voting papers are accompanied by election addresses, as few schools will be able to guarantee the accuracy of the translations.

The new parent governor

The parent governor will have informed views as to whether the head and the school successfully put policy into practice. As a recipient of newsletters and other correspondence from the school, they will also have views on the effectiveness of the communication systems.

Their first official visit is an opportunity for a tour of the school to meet the staff and to see the children at work. The parent governor will probably

know the teachers who have taught their own children, but have little knowledge of other members of staff.

During the tour, take the opportunity to focus on a number of aspects of management and curriculum, including the importance of children's talk in class as opposed to total silence, the development of handwriting skills, the emphasis on display work, the maintenance of good behaviour, and the value of practical activities.

Keep an album of recent photographs in the headteacher's room to illustrate the extracurricular activities which take place and the ways in which educational visits form a vital part of the curriculum. Over a well-earned cup of coffee on completion of the tour, the new governor can browse through the album, and the head can check that they have received booklets on the role of governors and information about courses from the LEA.

At the end of the first official visit to the school, the new parent governor should go away feeling that there is a positive contribution to be made, and that their contribution will be appreciated.

Keeping governors informed

Badly informed governors are more likely to make bad decisions. So it is in the school's best interests to make sure that governors are well-acquainted with the school, its staff and its children.

Invitations to school plays, carol concerts, assemblies, sports days, and so on, are not enough. If governors are to form a realistic and balanced impression of the school, they need to see more than the 'showcase events'. They need to know how the curriculum is organised, delivered and received, and to gain some first-hand knowledge of life in the classroom.

If they find it impossible to visit during the school day, you could make video tapes of classroom activities and loan them out to governors. Members of staff should regularly be invited to address governors' meetings about aspects of the curriculum and their special responsibilities within the school.

The governors' meeting

The governors' meeting can be quite intimidating for those parents who have not previously been involved in committee work.

The staffroom is probably the best place to hold the meeting, with easy chairs arranged in an informal way to help create a relaxed atmosphere.

It is important to provide the governors with visual evidence that the school is achieving its aims and objectives. Use displays of children's work and photographs of their activities arranged around the room to illustrate points made in reports by members of staff. These reports should be written in plain language, unavoidable technical terms being explained clearly but not in a patronising way.

The style and content of a report suitable for an in-service course or conference is unlikely to be appropriate for a governors' meeting. One headteacher has been known to read a 24-page report on young children's language development to bemused governors!

Staff appointments

Perhaps the most important task that governors undertake is the appointment of senior staff to the school. But parent governors in particular will probably have no relevant training or experience.

To ensure fair play, the headteacher should provide information and impartial guidance to the interview panel. At an early stage all governors will need to see the job descriptions and further particulars supplied to candidates. On the day of the appointment they should be given an opportunity to meet at the school before the interviews to see copies of the application forms of the short-listed candidates, to agree on the sorts of qualities they are looking for, and to plan the roles they are each to play in the interviews. A duplicated assessment form can be useful for new governors.

INTERVIEW ASSESSMENT FORM

NAME	APPLICATION FORM	REFERENCE	INTERVIEW	COMMENTS
PHYSICAL Appearance Speech				
EXPERIENCE & QUALIFICATIONS Initial training In-service training Range of experience Specialist knowledge				
INTELLIGENCE Evidence of – grasp of ideas – an ability to express ideas – sense of purpose				
PERSONAL QUALITIES Adaptability Communication Enthusiasm Persistence Reliability Leadership Sense of humour				

A check-list for parent governor involvement

• Are parent governors regularly invited to the school to learn at first hand what teachers and ancillary workers are doing and trying to develop?

• Are parent governors encouraged to learn what others in the locality think about the school, and to put them right if they are misinformed?

• Are all governors encouraged to take an interest in the children by 'adopting' a specific age group or aspect of the curriculum for a set period, and then reporting back informally at the governors' meeting?

• Do all governors receive copies of letters to parents as a matter of routine?

• Are parent governors encouraged to keep the headteacher and staff aware of potential trouble brewing?

• Are parent governors consulted at an early stage about potential changes in the curriculum?

• Are parent governors encouraged to mobilise public support on specific issues?

• Are parent governors always clear about the implications of implementing policies that are likely to be controversial (eg anti-racism, sex education and work to reduce stereotyping)?

• Are all parents aware of the purpose and functions of the governing body? Are the addresses of governors displayed prominently around the school so that contact by other parents can be made easily?

• How should the parent governors provide feedback to other parents? What assistance should the school provide in this?

• What should be the relationship between the parent governors and formal parent groups?

Chapter Eight

The parents' evening

There are four main perspectives on parents' evenings. The first is that of the headteacher: 'A good turn-out — 93 per cent — it's amazing what a bit of positive encouragement does.'

The second belongs to the senior sages of the staffroom: 'Of course, you never actually see those that you really want to see.'

The third is the parents' perspective — apprehensive confused and guilty: apprehensive about what 'they' are going to say; confused by the vague generalities of the professional ('What exactly am I supposed to do?'); and guilty about not providing the background, time and encouragement that all children need and few have.

The fourth perspective belongs to the children, judged and sentenced in their absence: 'What did she say, Mum?'

Are we locked up too tightly in our own perceptions and with our own preoccupations to recognise that contact with parents, particularly on parents' evenings, is often worthless and sometimes even harmful? It's very easy for headteachers to play the numbers game, focusing on the quantity rather than the quality of the encounters.

All teachers want to be, and seen to be, caring, concerned, knowledgeable, hard-working professionals. But is this the image projected at parents' evenings? Is care reflected in the quality of the display of children's work in classrooms and around the school? Does our concern extend to ensuring a well-run appointments system and consultations that are carried out with some degree of privacy?

Do all members of the school's staff work hard to ensure that the parents end up with a greater understanding of their children's education and with positive views about the school?

Senior staff should be asking why some parents don't respond eagerly to parents' evening invitations. If the evening is seen as an opportunity for the teacher to moan about the shortcomings of the children, then who can blame parents for not returning year after year for more of the same treatment? Also, to be asked directly, 'Well, what do you think?' unsettles the most confident and articulate parent. The question presupposes that the parent understands why the work was done, what it aimed to achieve, and how it fitted into the scheme of work. The teacher may well know all this, but the parent probably won't. A much better opening question is: 'Have you noticed the improvement in . . . ?'

There are ways of finding starting points for co-operation and collaboration. The teacher can, for example, point out that John can't tell the time and that most of his friends can. 'Why don't we try to teach him to tell the time by the end of next term?' would be a fine start to planning a joint programme. Setting shared short-term targets for parent, teacher and child should be an important aspect of any consultation.

If the parents' evening is at an inconvenient time for particular parents due to shift work, the lack of baby-sitters, family illness or a whole range of other causes, make separate individual appointments.

How do parents' evenings affect children? Too often the teacher's carefully chosen words can be misunderstood or taken out of context. What is the child to do when an irate parent returns from parents' evening to clip him round the head and tell him to work harder? How does the child interpret 'work'? For instance, if the child spends a lot of time at school colouring, in order to reinforce valuable knowledge or experience, will 'working harder' at colouring have the desired effect? In order to strive harder, the child needs to have the target clearly identified.

Timing

A parents' evening held early in the school year provides an opportunity for teachers to update and verify the information held in school. It is also an opportunity for parents and teachers to weigh each other up, and for the teacher to reassure parents about their interest and concern for individual children. Both parents and teachers can share their expectations for the children, and explore ways of working collaboratively to fulfil these expectations if possible.

A parents' evening held about half-way through the spring term provides a chance to review progress and to revise and renegotiate the system of mutual support.

A meeting held towards the end of the school year gives time to review progress, but there is little opportunity to rectify misunderstandings or, if the child is to change classes, to build on the achievements made during the year.

Reminders for parents' evening
Parents must be convinced that the staff are doing a good job in educating and caring for their child. The parents are vitally interested in the performance of their child, and not necessarily interested in the school as an institution or in other children.

• Parents are customers — if they don't like the service your school offers, they will go elsewhere. Not only will they take their own children, but they may take their neighbours' children too!

• Be patient and pleasant, and listen to what parents have to say. Teachers sometimes use techniques on parents which would be more suited to children, or even adopt an authoritarian approach that discourages any form of worthwhile dialogue.

• If parents anticipate that nothing very positive will be said about their child, they may well be defensive or even aggressive. It is essential to start and finish an interview with positive and encouraging remarks.

• Parents can't be expected to solve teachers' problems. If the children's work is untidy, if they shout out in lessons, or if they can't spell, the problem is the teacher's.

• Brief notes should be made before the meeting, and exercise books, folders, and other pieces of work should be available to illustrate comments on performance and development.

• The meeting is an opportunity to exchange information, so teachers can also take an interest in what children do outside school.

• Information held in the school's

records should be verified and updated by parents. It is a good idea to hold a staff meeting after the parents' evening to update and share relevant information, particularly on health matters, since staff may need to be aware of specific medical conditions.

• The staff need to encourage purposeful and informative dialogue with parents.

A check-list of questions for parents' evening

QUESTION	ACTION	DEVELOPMENT
Are there signs of improvement in reading, maths, writing and other curriculum areas?	Evidence to support judgement — children's work files, test results, exercise books.	Encourage parental involvement.
Is my child having difficulties in reading, writing, maths? Are you making any special provision to help with these difficulties?	Evidence Special group work with special educational needs.	Encourage parental help with specific tasks.
What is my child good at? What are you doing to encourage those strengths?	Evidence	Encourage parental involvement and praise. Possibly encourage involvement with outside groups.
How does the standard of my child's work compete with the rest of the class?	Evidence	Encourage parental involvement. Offer reassurance if justified.

What is my child's attitude to work?	Discuss motivation.	Focus on tasks that motivate, excite and challenge.
How does my child relate to other children and adults at school?	Discuss friendship groups, inquire about behaviour at home.	Encourage involvement.
What topics are going to be covered during the next few weeks	Outline plans for the period.	Encourage support and involvement.

Organisation

One model of organisation for parents' evenings which works well is given below.

• The date of the parents' evening is agreed by all staff at a staff meeting, at least one term in advance.

• Parents are given about six weeks' notice of the forthcoming parents' evening, perhaps as an item in a regular newsletter.

• A staff meeting is held to finalise arrangements, and to run through the points listed earlier on purposes and processes.

• Two weeks before the parents' evening a general invitation is sent to the parents giving the date, purpose, range of times available, crèche facilities, and a request that parents come into school to sign up for an appointment on sheets displayed in the entrance hall.

• Colourful notices are put up around the school encouraging parents to sign up.

• Two days before the date, personal reminders are sent to those parents who have not signed.

Dear

I notice that you have not signed up for an appointment for parents' evening on .... I wonder if you would like to come and see me at .... ?

If you can't make that evening, perhaps you would be able to pop in and see me after school on ......

Yours sincerely

• On the evening, the headteacher keeps on the move, checking that all is running smoothly, and encouraging parents to have a quiet word if they have concerns which they wish to discuss.

Keep a record of parents attending parents' evenings, and use alternative approaches, such as home visiting, to bridge the communication gap with those who don't attend.

Parents and matters of discipline

In all schools the behaviour and conduct of children is governed by rules. These are usually quite simple and often little more than the application of common sense and courtesy. It isn't necessary to carve them on tablets of stone, and usually they are not recorded on paper.

It is inevitable that these rules will be broken, and when the infringement is minor, a quiet word and a wagged finger are often enough.

However, occasionally one or two children will become involved in behaviour which is positively antisocial and perhaps even illegal. Circumstances will dictate the action to be taken on these occasions, but as a general rule it is best to invite the parents into the school to discuss what has happened and the course of action to be taken.

It is important to show support for the parent and child as well as concern over the wrong-doing, so that discussion can be positive and constructive. Listen to what the parents have to say before

outlining your own proposals; modifying decisions and statements as new facts become known creates the impression of 'woolly-mindedness' and indecision.

It may sometimes be necessary to involve educational welfare officers, educational psychologists or even social service workers in order to reach an effective solution to a particular problem.

A school which has developed strong positive links with individual parents has a greater chance of dealing successfully with difficult situations. When parents are welcomed as regular visitors to the school, early signs of a potential problem can be discussed, and a co-operative strategy agreed and brought into operation.

Chapter Nine

Special needs

The range of children needing special provision in primary schools extends from those with minor learning problems or physical disability to those with needs which, at one time, would have been met by a special school placement.

Few would argue against the policy of integrating children with special educational needs into mainstream schools, given the adequate provision of suitable equipment, facilities and staffing.

The school and parents should resist the temptation to place a child in a mainstream school until appropriate and adequate resources are in place.

The parents of these children play a crucial role in helping the school to make an effective contribution to the child's education.

The rights of both children and parents are recognised in the 1981 Education Act, which compels LEAs to prepare individual statements of needs and how the LEA will meet those needs. Formal consultation, feedback and review are built into the statementing system, but the involvement of a number of agencies, including educational, psychological and health, makes the process a slow business. Additional close contact between school and parents is essential to ensure a rapid and effective response to needs and opportunities as they arise.

The Warnock Report, published in 1978, stressed that the full involvement of parents is necessary for the successful education of children with special educational needs.

As up to 20 per cent of children will have special educational needs at some time during their school career, it is vital that schools have a clearly thought-out policy on special needs provision, and the ways in which parents and support agencies can be involved in policy-making and implementation.

Children with learning difficulties

If a child has a learning difficulty which is significantly greater than that of the majority of children of the same age, and the LEA decides that the child has special educational needs, provision should be made in ordinary schools subject to:

- parents' views,
- the ability of the school to meet the child's needs,
- efficient use of resources.

There are children who have needs which cannot be adequately met by the local school and should therefore be educated in a special school where appropriate facilities are available. Transfer is not done solely at the request of the mainstream school; the referral and assessment procedure is necessarily thorough, the parents and a number of agencies being consulted at each stage.

There have been, in the recent past, attempts by some schools to use suspension as a way of short-circuiting the normal procedures for referral for special education. Suspending a child from a primary school for a place in a special school puts both the parents and the child at a disadvantage. The assessment process is conducted when the child's education has been most severely disrupted, and parents are presented with a *fait accompli*, since the mainstream school has already washed its hands of any responsibility for the child.

It goes without saying that all children are special and have specific as well as general needs. However, some children's needs arise from physical, intellectual or emotional conditions which require particular attention, and demand the input of expertise that isn't normally available on a daily basis within mainstream schools.

Earlier chapters have suggested ways to encourage parents to help their children with language development, maths, project work and other curriculum areas. With the relationship between home and school focusing on the needs and capabilities of the individual child, it is vitally important to set targets, share ideas and offer reassurance.

All LEAs have specialist services to which parents and schools can turn to for advice and guidance. These usually include psychologists, physiotherapists and experts on visual and hearing handicaps. It is essential that parents and schools know about these services and apply to them for advice. A list of specialist organisations and associations can be found on pages 141-144.

Specialist equipment may be needed for those children with physical handicaps, and the LEA should be made aware of these needs by school and

parents. If specialist peripatetic staff are working with children with special needs in school, arrangements should be made for these teachers to be available on parents' evenings.

Schools make provision for those with intellectual difficulties in various ways. Parents should be aware of any special arrangements made for their children. If children are withdrawn from classes for additional help in basic subjects then parents should be told. They also should be told about the sorts of work the remainder of the class undertake during those periods and the steps taken to ensure that their children's education remains broad and balanced.

Children with special abilities

Children with special abilities include those with exceptional intellectual and/or physical skills. Children with musical, gymnastic or sporting potential may need specialist teaching which is not fully catered for by the normal curriculum of the school. It would be shameful if the potential of these children was not developed and their special abilities nurtured.

Children with theatrical or dancing talents sometimes need to take time off school for auditions and performances. Close contact must be maintained between home and school over these breaks in attendance to make sure that the momentum of school-based learning is maintained and that vital stages in learning are not missed.

Exceptionally bright children can pose particular problems, in the classroom and at home, unless suitable demanding and interesting challenges are presented.

The Plowden Report pointed out that there is an 'egalitarian suspicion of the whole concept of giftedness', although it is universally admitted that 'gifted' people do exist. If teachers are unsympathetic to the special needs of such children, their school life can become quite miserable.

The task of the parents and the school is to create an environment where these children can flourish, while still maintaining a fair balance in the distribution of time, interest and material resources for other children in the family and school.

Help is at hand through the work of the National Association for Gifted Children, which not only provides advice and guidance to parents through newsletters and other publications, but also has an extensive network of local groups which provide contacts for parents and arrange activities for children. (LEA advisers may also be able to suggest suitable contacts for parents.)

Some of these local groups organise regular clubs, at which children meet others with similar talents and abilities, make friends and extend their interests together. The children are not required to pass any form of test to attend, and their brothers and sisters are encouraged to take part as well.

A sense of perspective and proportion is given to parents by the association through the following advice: 'Whatever form of exceptional ability a child may show, the best preparation for growing up is to have lived fully as a child. Accelerating mental development or a particular talent is sometimes bought at the expense of slowing down the pace of social and emotional growth, and the result can be an uneven and maladjusted individual. There are times when a child, however clever, will want to play and act like other children, and he or she should be encouraged to do so.'

Chapter Ten

Home visiting

This chapter examines ways in which schools and teachers directly extend their influence to the home. This can be a sensitive area, since good intentions can easily become counter-productive, but with a clear sense of purpose and determination, good, solid results can be achieved.

Traditionally it is the school attendance officers, education welfare officers and school nurses who visit parents at home, usually to warn, reprimand or offer strong but sometimes unwelcome advice. Such visits may be prompted by a child's poor attendance at school, truancy, headlice or poor standards of personal cleanliness.

However, a new kind of home visiting has recently emerged. Teachers in some schools have taken the initiative in home-school relationships by visiting parents themselves in an effort to establish closer links between parents and schools. This happens more in infant, first and nursery schools and, to a lesser degree, with teachers of younger junior children.

Home-school liaison teachers

A number of LEAs have appointed home-school liaison teachers in urban areas. Through a regular timetable commitment, the teacher establishes strong links with parents, particularly those with pre-school children and children with special educational needs.

The purpose of visiting parents of pre-school children is to explain what goes on in nursery and reception classes. Often the teacher takes along a small pack of material prepared in the school for the parents to use with the child. This may include a general information booklet about the school, booklets on story-telling, number games, and general activity books.

Home visiting not only gives the teacher a chance to prepare parents and children for the activities and behaviour to be expected at school, but also gives parents a chance to ask questions. In the security of their own home, parents are more likely to talk about concerns they might have with supporting their child's learning due to problems of health, unemployment, poverty, overcrowding or the parents' own level of literacy. The home-school liaison teacher may be able to suggest or establish links with appropriate agencies to help with particular problems.

The purpose of involving parents through direct contact is to encourage support rather than apportion blame for poor progress.

Very often the parents that teachers really want to meet on parents' evening are those who don't turn up, so one of the tasks of home visiting is to arrange visits to the school for those parents who are reluctant to respond to written invitations.

Another important aspect of the role is to establish and maintain strong links with nurseries and voluntary groups within the local area.

The liaison teacher could release other teachers from classes on a regular basis, so that they too can make a contribution to working with parents. This sort of arrangement ensures that the liaison teacher keeps teaching skills sharp and is fully involved with curriculum development within the school.

Priorities

It is vitally important that the home-school liaison teacher, or any other member of staff who visits parents at home, reports back to colleagues at school. This helps to correct misconceptions, and avoids stereotyped and inaccurate views about the families that their school serves. Both staff and parents must be convinced that the work of the home-school liaison teacher is an effective and efficient use of teacher time. They need to be satisfied that this time would not be better spent on working with groups of children in classes, or even in meeting groups of parents at school.

Not all teachers will be sympathetic to the idea of home visiting. They may believe that there should be a line of demarcation between the worlds of home and school: that parents are entitled to some privacy and freedom to bring up their children without undue and uninvited pressure from schools, and that teachers and children need some privacy away from the pressure of parents to establish relationships, trust and rapport.

Unless teachers are strongly committed to the principle of parental involvement in education, they should not be involved in a home visiting programme.

If the programme of home visiting lacks clear objectives and tight planning, coupled with an adequate means of communication, it can be perceived by critics as little more than social chit-chat and a way of retrieving unreturned reading books!

Monday 4th

Dear

I'm visiting some parents tomorrow, and I'd like to pop in and see you at about ten o'clock to chat about . . . . . .

Please let me know if you won't be in.

Yours sincerely,

Arranging visits

An out-of-the-blue knock on the door and 'just happened to be in the street so I thought I'd pop in to see you', is a style of approach used by some home-school liaison teachers, which has the advantages of flexibility over the use of time and spontaneity. On the other hand, parents can be caught at a disadvantage, half-way through a 'spring clean' or just off to the shops.

However, providing parents with advance warning also presents difficulties, as they will naturally be concerned over the purpose of the visit and perhaps feel that they, or their children, have been singled out for special attention. A hand-written note in a friendly tone rather than a typed letter in official prose will help to prepare parents for the visit without making them feel threatened.

Families in difficulty

A teacher may receive indications at school that a family is in difficulty. Frequent or prolonged unexplained absence from school, non-payment of dinner money or money for a class trip, a sudden deterioration in a child's performance or behaviour — all these suggest that something is amiss and that a visit would be worthwhile.

The home visit shouldn't be a snooping expedition, but if home conditions are such that children are seriously effected (eg essential services cut off through non-payment of bills, unhygienic conditions, no food in the house) then the appropriate agencies need to be contacted.

Extreme caution must be exercised by the school over information given by other parents. It is often difficult to

distinguish between malicious gossip
and reliable information given through
genuine concern.

Children at risk

If a teacher suspects that a child is being
sexually abused, the school must
immediately set in motion the
procedures laid down by the LEA; there
can be no discretionary action. Where
guidelines don't exist, a senior officer of
the LEA and/or the schools' medical
officer should be contacted straight away
by phone for guidance and direction.

All children collect bruises, cuts, grazes
and scratches as part of growing up.
Accidents happen to children at home as
they do in the playground and classroom.
However, if there is a suspicion of non-
accidental injury, then again LEA
procedures need to be set in motion
urgently.

Chapter Eleven

Fund-raising

It is a fact of life that LEA allowances to schools barely cover the cost of even the most basic items of consumable stock. Therefore schools face a dilemma: they can use just the monies provided from central funds and lobby hard until adequate funding is provided; or they can attempt to raise funds from an additional source, invariably the parents, to replace expensive items or to add to the resources already available.

Some schools have little difficulty in raising money. The parents are willing and able to dig deep into their pockets to finance the most ambitious schemes. However, in less prosperous areas, schools are well aware of the financial hardship of many families, and are reluctant to put even more pressure on limited resources. After all, it is more important that the children are adequately clothed and fed, than that another computer or a school minibus is provided.

According to the Advisory Centre for Education (ACE): 'Experience from parents' groups around the country shows that the more parents try to fill the gaps in basic items the wider the gap grows between local schools. Some are just unable to raise the cash. The other lesson is that the more parents try to provide these items, the less pressure there is on the LEA to fulfil its duties and the easier it is for it to get parents to try to provide yet more essential items.'

The report by HMI, *LEA Provision for Education and the Quality of Response in Schools and Colleges in 1985*, shows that more than five per cent of primary schools gained at least twice as much as their capitation allowance through voluntary fund-raising activities.

Ideas for raising funds

Regular donations
Perhaps the simplest way of raising money is to ask families to contribute a fixed sum on a weekly or termly basis. Initially this can be quite successful, but over time support often dwindles and is difficult to regenerate.

Sponsored events
Sponsored events can be great cash generators, but restrictions on the amount pledged need to be written on the sponsor form to avoid resentment from supporters being asked to 'fork out' much more than they had anticipated.

Favourites include spelling lists, multiplication tables, fun runs, swimming and silences.

Parents' associations may find a sponsored 'slim' not only an incentive to raise money but also a worthwhile activity!

School fairs
With enough time to prepare, working parties of parents will produce all sorts of

merchandise for sale at a school fair. Try to find space for the working parties to meet at school, so that relationships are strengthened, and parents who would normally be hesitant about joining in committee work or working with children in the classroom, will come into school and realise that they can confidently contribute to the running of the school.

Parents will often, for a limited period, quite happily turn their homes into production centres for dolls' clothing, toffee apples, stuffed toys, toilet roll covers, etc. They are also usually helpful in organising and running stalls on the day.

Scholastic's *Crafty Moneymakers* in the *Bright Ideas* series is packed with useful suggestions (available from Scholastic Publications).

'Antique' auctions

Another useful fund-raiser is an 'antique' auction of items donated by parents and friends. If the event is well-advertised through posters around the neighbourhood and in the local press, a crowd of potential bidders could be drawn in from a wide area, many having no connection with the school.

The auctioneer's pace needs to be rapid and will need a light touch. Getting through the items quickly rather than hanging on for the last penny makes the event more lively and enjoyable.

Car boot sales

Car boot sales offer a chance of profit with minimum outlay. Check first with the local council trading officer, the school governors and the education office, since there may be local by-laws which prevent you from holding such an event on certain days and may also restrict the number that can be held within a given period.

Announce the sale in a number of newspapers within about a ten-mile radius of the school, stating the date, time, cost per pitch and a contact telephone number. All you need to do then is arrange some local community advertising, the running of refreshments, and the stocking and manning of a school stall, and collect the fees for the pitches.

Raffles

Raffles are also straightforward to run. Local traders may well contribute prizes, the butcher might be persuaded to provide a turkey at Christmas, the baker a cake, the greengrocer a basket of fruit, and so on. Make sure that a lottery licence is obtained from the local authority for anything more than a small raffle.

Coffee mornings

These provide a chance not only for parents to get together and meet each other in an informal setting, but also to raise a little money through the sale of refreshments and raffles.

General knowledge quizzes

General knowledge quizzes consisting of general questions and specialist rounds may unearth some budding local masterminds! An entry charge for teams can be redistributed as part of the prize money, while the sale of refreshments will maximise profits.

Discos, barn dances, 'rock and roll' nights

There is scope here for two types of event: whole family evenings or over-18s only with a licensed bar. A local pub may be willing to arrange bar facilities, including application for a licence, giving the school a percentage of the profits.

You may be able to make more money by running your own bar, but there is a great deal more work involved in hiring equipment, purchasing stock and manning the bar with volunteer staff.

Auctions of pledges and promises

Parents and friends may be persuaded to auction their services — nothing immoral, of course! For example, a half day of housework, a chance to fly in the company's aeroplane, window cleaning for a week, a bag of coal, etc, can all be pledged and auctioned off to the highest bidder.

Theatre companies and entertainers

Professional entertainers, including folk groups, comedians and specialist companies, will provide an evening's programme for the school. Profits will depend on whether the school pays the entertainers a fixed fee, no matter what the takings are, or gives a fixed percentage of the takings.

You could combine an entertainment with another event: for example, a 'magic and mystery evening' at Hallowe'en could include a fancy dress disco and a magician providing entertainment in an interval.

Bulk buy clubs

The 'home-school association' should be able to obtain trading facilities on a cash sale basis with wholesale warehouses. With a little prior planning and organisation, bulk quantities of merchandise, such as baked beans, toilet paper and disposable nappies, can also be obtained at a substantial discount for resale to parents, a percentage of the savings being donated to association funds.

Clothes-swap schemes

Children tend to outgrow rather than wear out clothes in the early years. A monthly exchange/sale gives parents an opportunity to save money while raising funds for the school.

Financial assistance from other organisations

Casting the net wider for help with specific projects within the school can often pay dividends. The local Rotary Club, the Women's Institute and commercial and industrial sponsors can usually be persuaded to contribute. There may also be charitable trusts administered by the LEA which can assist certain children to take part in school-organised camps and expeditions that would perhaps be too much of a strain on family funds. A phone call to the Education Office could reveal a source of help.

What shall we do with the money?

Many parents will readily support fund-raising activities for the school, giving little thought to the ways in which the money will be spent.

Most schools inform parents of the items bought from the funds raised, and many discuss specific targets with parent groups before fund-raising activities are planned. If parents have contributed to a major purchase or raised money for an addition or alteration to the school buildings, it is important to acknowledge their support. A thank-you letter to all parents is always appreciated.

A small, semi-official handing-over ceremony attended by the chairman of the governors and other VIPs would be worth considering. The local newspaper may welcome advance notice of the event and send along a photographer and reporter, providing useful publicity for the school.

Chapter Twelve

Projects involving parents

Environmental projects

Both children and parents could become involved in projects to improve the school environment and provide further learning opportunities. Building a school pond, making a nature trail and improving the playground are just a few ideas.

A school pond
A pond can be both an attractive feature and a valuable study area for any school, so why not create one with the help of parents?

In the initial planning stages, remember that safety is all important: the sides should shelve gently, the overall depth needs careful consideration, and there should be a paved area around the edge to provide a firm footing. (The local council are usually quite happy to provide a load of broken paving slabs which can be used to form a crazy paving edge around the pond.)

You will need to find an area no smaller than 18m — the bigger the better. Textbooks on the subject recommend a minimum depth of 38cm to prevent sharp changes in temperature which can make life uncomfortable for aquatic life. To ensure the safety of children it is sensible not to dig much deeper than this.

If one end of the pool tapers slightly, birds will flock to bathe and drink from the shallow end.

Concrete ponds will release lime, so they will need to be painted with Silglaze or some other neutralising agent to protect plants and fish.

Building a pond can be hard and heavy work, especially if you line it with concrete, since this will need mixing and it goes hard quite quickly.

Junior children can be involved in site planning and a variety of scientific and mathematical activities related to pond building, and the older children can help with the digging, too. Some of the parents may be shift-workers, able to give time to the project during the school day, while others may prefer to work on a weekend.

Given that most school grounds are easily accessible, the pond needs to be constructed from material strong enough to deter the efforts of the most determined vandal — a polythene liner may be suitable for a secure area, but can be quickly damaged beyond repair on an open site. To make a really strong pond lining, cover the polythene liner with a layer of wire mesh, then bury this under a thick layer of concrete.

A pond of even modest dimensions can demand a great deal of digging — a cubic metre of soil weighs well over a tonne. A group of parents can be invited to form a working party. With any luck, it will include at least one who is a builder, or who works in the construction industry, and has all the technical know-how needed.

Once the pond is finished and stocked with plants and water creatures, it must receive fairly regular attention or it could become an unsightly overgrown mess choked with litter.

Making a nature trail

If the school is lucky enough to possess a field, making a nature trail is fairly straightforward, with a little imagination, determination and energy.

Again, a working party of interested, committed parents is essential, since it is too much for one person to tackle on their own. If a pond has already been established, this would make a good starting point.

You could incorporate any of the following:

• The pond
This gives a home to tadpoles, frogs, toads, newts, pond skaters, dragon-fly nymphs, sticklebacks and a variety of plants. Parents will often provide stock from garden ponds.

• The drystone wall
A drystone wall provides a home for a variety of mini-beasts. To make the wall safe and secure, support it with an earth bank.

• Bird boxes
Attach bird boxes to trees and buildings. The RSPB will provide advice on the construction and siting of a number of boxes which are likely to attract a variety of birds.

• Young trees
Planting a variety of saplings will provide useful learning activities for children, but they will need help with digging and staking.

• Shrubs and bushes
Shrubs and bushes are also important, particularly those which attract butterflies and other insects. Buddleia is particularly attractive to butterflies. Make sure that none of the plants produce seeds which are harmful to children if eaten.

• Broken drain-pipes
The local public works department is

often willing to supply and deliver large broken drain-pipes. If these are partially buried they can make attractive dens for foxes, but take advice first!

- A log pile
A variety of mini-beasts will be attracted by creating a log pile. This will also provide a home for all sorts of fungi.

- Tree trunks
If the parks department are felling in the area, they will usually be quite happy to supply the school with large tree trunks. These need to be carefully secured to prevent them from being rolled. A variety of insects will make their homes under the bark, and wood-boring insects will burrow into the dead wood.

- A bog area
A large sheet of plastic buried below the surface will alter the drainage of a patch of ground. Rushes, mosses, ferns, primulas and irises will flourish in this sort of environment.

- A wild patch
A fenced-off area can be left to seed itself. (The groundsman responsible for the school will need to know that this area shouldn't be mown.)

- Markers
Suitable location markers need to be made and sited so that worksheets and workbooks have reference points.

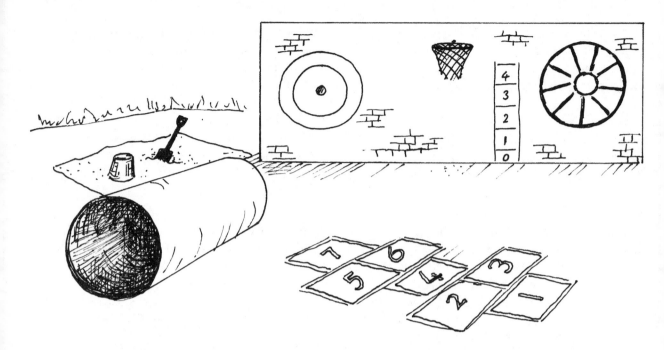

Making an interesting playground

Playgrounds usually consist of drab, uninteresting slabs of tarmac with, if the children are lucky, some sort of shelter or wind-break to offer just a little protection from the worst of the weather. Most modern schools don't even have a window-free piece of wall to kick or throw a ball against. It's no wonder that many children prefer to stay in classrooms and corridors at break-times rather than face such an arid landscape.

Even with a tight budget, the appearance of the playground can be transformed by a couple of tins of paint, a few brushes, a bit of imagination and a little help from parents.

Colourful hopscotch squares, number snakes and amazing mazes can 'miraculously' appear. Given enough room, games courts and even a roller skating rink can be marked out.

If wall space is available, paint targets for all sorts of ball games. A basket containing a fixed number of balls, skipping ropes and hoops could be provided for break-times. (Someone, preferably a child, needs to check that all have been returned at the end of break.)

If there isn't a suitable blank wall, why not ask the parents to build one? Building a wall is tricky, so advice and practical help from someone with knowledge and experience is essential to make sure that the structure will be both safe and reasonably attractive.

Parents could also help to construct a sand-pit at the edge of the playground. They will need to make a cover to keep the sand clean and to protect it from prowling cats and dogs.

The home-school association may be persuaded to provide funds for a few benches and some other items of playground furniture.

Large tree trunks acquired from the parks department, and sub-standard mains drainage pipes from the public works department, make excellent playground equipment but need to be bedded in so that they are completely stable and safe.

For a more challenging venture, parents could construct an adventure playground. This would be a major project in which the organisers of local MSC-funded work experience may also wish to be involved.

One of the problems of attractive and interesting outdoor structures is that they can act as a magnet to local vandals after school hours. So make sure the structures are substantial and robust.

Collecting material for a school museum

Children learn best from first-hand experience, and they are far more interested and excited by handling physical materials than learning from print.

Children cannot continually visit and revisit museums and places of historical interest to gain first-hand experience, but you could start a museum within the school.

Parents can be approached to help to equip the museum. Clearing attics and tidying out sheds and garages often uncovers interesting 'treasures' from the recent past.

Photographs of classes and school reports from years gone by, photographs of the neighbourhood, old newspapers and comics, gas masks and ration books, pre-decimal coins, and even chimney-sweeping brushes help to create a feeling for the past. To make the whole exercise even more interesting, try to persuade the donors of the material to visit the school and be interviewed by the children.

Home assignments, surveys and interviews

An earlier chapter looked at homework, focusing mainly on subjects and specific tasks, but homework could also take the form of an extended project.

One of the advantages of an extended project is that it is a shared activity, another focal point for conversation between parents and child. It need not be an activity where the parent already knows all the answers, but as parents and children work together the project will take on a life of its own and head in all sorts of unexpected directions. Extended projects should not be seen merely as a way of keeping children quietly occupied, demanding no adult interest or intervention.

Listed below are some examples of extended assignments taken from the Schools' Council working paper 75, *Primary Practice: a Sequel to the Practical Curriculum* (Methuen Education), which have been successful with children aged eight to eleven.
• Collecting examples of trade marks in connection with a class project on 'Heraldry'.
• Locating different road signs for subsequent art work on symmetry in the environment.
• Pinpointing the location of local police stations, hospitals and fire stations for subsequent location on a map of the area.

- Tracing the family tree in relation to work on 'Heredity'.
- Collecting, identifying and pressing some leaves as part of some project work on 'Trees'.
- Finding out where all known relatives live and where they were born to help the class examine how family members spread geographically.
- Locating unusual notices and plaques in the environs ('things we see but never notice').
- Collecting different types of lettering from magazines and newspapers to help develop various formats for some illuminated lettering work.
- Logging details of a family outing or journey for the subsequent construction of travel graphs, and speed calculations.

Making a family history book
The 'family tree' idea can be extended to make a family history book based on a questionnaire developed by the children on the following lines:

- Where did Grandad/Grandma work?
- What did they do?
- What did they earn?
- How old were they when they left school?
- Where did they live when they were young?
- How did they travel from place to place?
- What did they do when they were aged eight/nine/ten/eleven?
- What did they wear?
- What did they like to eat?
- What sorts of toys did they have?
- What sorts of games did they play?
- Do we know anything about their parents?

The book could be illustrated with maps, drawings, newspaper clippings and family photographs.

Sensitivity and tact are important when setting work on the topic of

families, since a number of children in a classroom may not have straightforward family backgrounds.

Holiday journey
Children could be involved in the excitement of planning the family holiday. Through using maps and road atlases of different scales they can find the best route, and can then calculate distances and identify suitable rest stops. The children can also take some responsibility for what they take with them on the holiday, making lists of what they will need.

After the holiday they could fill a scrapbook with postcards, photographs and descriptions of the highlights, suitably illustrated and captioned: 'A drawing of Mum beside the mountain of sandwiches she made for the journey', 'On the M6 Dad had to get out all the cases to reach the spare tyre', 'This is a drawing of the crab I caught'.

Garden safari
Suggest that parents help their children to keep a record over a set period, showing animal, bird and insect visitors to the garden. This could include bird counts, evidence of foxes, squirrels, hedgehogs, drawings of mini-beasts, lists and drawings of plants and trees, along with attempts at making the garden more attractive to a wide range of wildlife.

Reporting back
Sharing with others the knowledge and achievements gained through a home assignment is vital. Showing the work and talking about it to classmates and the teacher helps to develop the project's learning potential to the full.

The 'why', 'what', 'where', 'when' and 'how' questions will not only inform the questioners but also sharpen up the understanding and perceptions of the child being questioned.

Children may even be willing to report back on their project to a wider audience during a school assembly.

Chapter Thirteen

Training teachers

It is surprising that some of the major preoccupations of teachers and schools — the 3Rs of relationships, routines and regulations — have only been of marginal interest to teacher trainers, policy makers and administrators. But the angry vocal parent at the classroom door, the boy who has left his swimming costume at home yet again, and finding time to put away all that junk collected for the jumble, are issues which push curriculum matters lower in the teacher's order of priority. These typical day-to-day crises can sometimes dominate life in the classroom, but go unnoticed by those outside.

Difficulties caused by misunderstandings between school and home are usually dealt with by schools and groups of parents in isolation, but training for work with parents has been almost non-existent. Working with parents is not always easy and good teachers are not necessarily extrovert or even particularly good at communicating with adults.

Pre-service courses

There should be a place for systematic training on initial training courses where students are given the opportunity to see schools and teachers from the parents' perspective.

Most probationary primary teachers are in direct informal contact with parents from their very first day with a class. Often it's just a matter of weeks before a more formal parents' evening arises and advice is sought and given on a range of professional matters; in most cases, probationer teachers are ill-prepared for this important facet of their work. Research has shown that one third of our primary teachers and roughly half of our secondary-trained teachers get little or no preparation for work with parents.

Our system of initial and in-service training has failed to give due regard to the importance of developing the appropriate attitudes, interpersonal skills and strategies necessary to recognise and tap into the vast reservoir of parental support available.

Janet Aitken and John Bastiani of Nottingham University have identified a number of key elements for the preparation of a pre-service training course:
1 A taught element — learning through study and research.
2 Supervised participation in school-based home/school programmes.
3 Additional experience of working alongside parents in a variety of settings.
4 College-based workshops using real and simulated materials so that the practical skills of listening and writing to parents become developed.

The skills needed for home visiting would be explored, and work on case-study and case-conference materials was also suggested.

It was emphasised that the elements of such a course should be planned as a coherent whole.

Starting a school-based inset programme

First review the work already being done, and look for ways to improve matters.

1 List the measures already taken by the school to involve parents in children's learning.

2 How are parents informed about the curriculum?

3 How effective is the system of written communication between school and home?

4 How successful are the arrangements for parents' evenings? What efforts are made to keep in touch with those parents who fail to attend the meetings?

5 How does the school carry out the registration and induction of children and families who are new to the school?

6 In what ways are parents encouraged to develop their children's learning at home? How is this linked to the work of the classroom, and what methods are used to provide parents with feedback?

7 Are parents encouraged to help around the school? How are they recruited?

8 Are parents encouraged to work in classrooms?

9 How are parents of children from minority groups involved?

10 Is there a home-school association? Who takes the initiative in its activities?

11 How can we improve what we already do? (The main difference between a good school and an excellent school seems to be that the excellent school does the same things just that little bit better.)

12 What new initiative should the school develop?

By visiting other schools, teachers can see how others are tackling parental involvement. The local primary adviser should be able to recommend places where good practice is being undertaken.

Focus attention on specifics and pose fairly probing but friendly questions; otherwise only vague, superficial impressions are likely to be formed.

It is useful for teachers to visit in pairs so that they can share perspectives. If different pairs of teachers are sent to the same school over a number of weeks, a set of contrasting views are likely to be formed. Invite the headteacher and members of the host school back to attend a staff meeting, so that in-depth questions can be asked, impressions put in context and ideas clarified.

Often those with specialist expertise will be willing to address staff meetings about their work. Members of the Community Education Development Centre could be invited to give talks, and even lecturers in marketing at the local polytechnic could talk about the strategies of hard/soft sell employed by commercial organisations — after all, if we are not selling the virtues of education, then what are we doing? Community directors from local community schools and evening institutes will talk about the sorts of work that they are undertaking in the neighbourhood, and may be able to suggest collaborative work.

Centre-based in-service courses

Examination of the details of management courses for headteachers,

deputies and senior post-holders also shows a concentration on curriculum and staff development. The skills needed to work with parents and the ways in which parents can help with children's learning are neglected.

Current trends in Government thinking seem to apportion to parents a judgemental role in schooling rather than that of partner and collaborator, and see the accountability of schools to parents as the major issue in parental involvement. The annual report by governors of schools to parents, and recent legislation increasing the proportion of parents on governing bodies, are evidence of this trend.

However, attendance figures at annual meetings, particularly when compared to attendance at the more traditional parents' evenings, show a lack of parental enthusiasm and support for the judgemental role.

Teachers, particularly heads, through legislative demands, now have to give a great deal of time and attention to accountability, and issues raised on training courses reflect a preoccupation with the ways in which schools can efficiently and effectively discharge these formal obligations.

Important and urgent as these issues may be, they do tend to deflect attention from the kinds of work with parents which have provided the main theme of this book.

Resources

Useful publications

The Government and Management of Schools G Baron and D A Howell (Athlone Press).

Written Communication Between Home and School John Bastiani (Publications Unit, University of Nottingham, University Park, Nottingham NG7 2RD).

Your Home School Links John Bastiani (New Education Press Ltd, 27 Old Gloucester Street, London WC1N 3XX).

Educational Administration ed K Brooksbank (Councils and Education Press Ltd).

School Governors: a Handbook of Guidance for Governors of County and Voluntary Schools K Brooksbank and J Revell (Councils and Education Press Ltd, Longman Group Ltd).

The Governor's Guide B Bullivant (Home and School Council, address below).

The School Governor's Handbook and Training Scheme T Burgess and A Sofer (Kogan Page).

Print — How You Can Do It Yourself (op) (Interaction, 15 Wilkin Street, London NW5).

Resources for Multicultural Education: an Introduction G Klein (Longman Resources Unit, 62 Hallfield Road, Oayerthorpe, York YO3 7XQ).

How to Run Committees and Meetings M Locke (Macmillan).

LEA (UK) Resources Centres and Contacts: Teachers' Guide (Multi-racial Education Resources Centre, c/o Denbigh Junior School, Denbigh Road, Luton LU3 1NS).

Governing Schools Starter Pack (P970) (The Open University, Learning Materials Service, Centre for Continuing Education, PO Box 188, Milton Keynes MK7 6VH). The Open University also runs a comprehensive course called *Governing Schools.*

The School in its Setting: a Guide to the Education Service for School Governors and Managers J Sallis (Advisory Centre for Education, address below).

The Effective School Governor J Sallis (Advisory Centre for Education).

School Prospectus Planning Kit F Taylor (Advisory Centre for Education).

ILEA Primary Catalogue (Marketing and Publicity Section, Television and Publishing Centre, Thackeray Road, London SW8).

A Handbook for School Governors E C Wragg and J A Partington (Methuen).

op Book is out of print; try libraries.

Useful addresses

Advisory Centre for Education (ACE), 18 Victoria Park Square, London E2 9PB. ACE provides useful advice and guidance for parents and teachers on a variety of educational matters. ACE also produces regular journal and information sheets on important topics including *Children with Special Needs: Sources of Help, ACE Special Education Handbook, Under 5s with Special Needs, Summary of 1981 Education Act,* and *Summary of the Warnock Report.*

Association of Blind and Partially Sighted Teachers and Students, The Secretary, British Monomark, Box 6727, London WC1N 3XX.

Association for Brain Damaged Children, Mrs Ann Roe (Secretary), 47 Northumberland Road, Coventry CV1 3AP.

Association for All Speech-Impaired Children (AFASIC), 347 Central Markets, Smithfield, London EC1A 9NH.

Association for Research into Restricted Growth, Miss Rosemary Ford (Secretary), 8 Herbert Road, Clevedon, Avon.

Association for Spina Bifida and Hydrocephalus (ASBAH), 22 Upper Woburn Place, London WC1H 0EP.

Asthma Society and Friends of Asthma Research Council, 300 Upper Street, London N1 2XX.

Breakthrough Trust Deaf Hearing Integration, Charles W Gillett Centre, Bristol Road, Selly Oak Colleges, Birmingham B29 6LE.

British Diabetic Association, 10 Queen Anne Street, London W1M 0BD.

British Dyslexia Association, 98 London Road, Reading RG1 5AU.

British Educational Management and Administration Society, 1 Lincoln's Inn Fields, London WC2.

British Epilepsy Association, Anstey House, 40 Hanover Square, Leeds LS3 1BE.

British Epilepsy Association (Scotland), 48 Govan Road, Glasgow G51 1JL.

Brittle Bones Society, Unit 4, Block 20, Carlunie Road, Dundee DD2 3QT.

Campaign for the Advancement of State Education, Sue Hodgson (Secretary), The Grove, High Street, Hawston, Cambridge CB2 4HT.

Centre for Studies on Integration in Education (CSIE), Spastics Society, Education Division, 1st Floor, 840 Brighton Road, Purley, Surrey CR2 2BH.

Chest, Heart and Stroke Association, The Welfare Society, Tavistock House North, Tavistock Square, London WC1H 9JE.

Child Poverty Action Group, 1–5 Bath Street, London EC1V 9PY. The group monitors the effect of government policies on the welfare of disadvantaged children and parents.

Children's Legal Centre, 20 Crompton Terrace, London N1 2UN. A watchdog organisation for children's legal rights. Particularly involved in immigration issues concerning the separation of parents and children.

Community Education Development Centre, Briton Road, Coventry CV2 4LF. Publications include *Going Community, Mother and Toddler Groups, Education Visiting, Nurseries and Parents, Parents in Partnership, Perspectives on Pre-school Home Visiting, Parents in the Primary School, Parents in the Classroom, Playaway Packs,* and *Early Years* (child development materials for parents). The centre also hires out films and video tapes. Publication order form available from Briton Road. A monthly newspaper and the quarterly *Journal of Community Education* are also available on request.

Cystic Fibrosis Research Trust, Alexandra House, 5 Blyth Road, Bromley, Kent BR1 3RS.

Down's Children's Association, 12–13 Clapham Common Southside, London SW4 7AA.

Gingerbread, 35 Wellington Street, London WC2E 7BN. Local self-help groups for single parents.

Greater London Federation of Parent-Teacher Associations, D Backhouse (Secretary), 20 Airley Gardens, Ilford, Essex IG1 GLB.

Home and School Council, Mrs Barbara Bullivant (Secretary), 81 Rustlings Road, Sheffield S11 7AB.

Evelina Children's Heart Organisation (ECHO), Mrs B Goddard (Membership Secretary), 52 Goddington Lane, Orpington, Kent BR6 9DS.

Haemophilia Society, 123 Westminster Bridge Road, London SE1 7HR.

Invalid Children's Aid Association, Alan Grahan House, 198 City Road, London EC1V 2PH.

Leukaemia Care Society, PO Box 82, Exeter, Devon EX2 5DP.

Multiple Sclerosis Society, 25 Effie Road, Fulham, London SW6 1EE.

Muscular Dystrophy Group of Great Britain, Natrass House, 35 Macaulay Road, Clapham, London SW4 0QP.

National Association for Mental Health (MIND), 22 Harley Street, London W1N 2ED.

National Association of Governors and Managers Educational Trust, 10 Brookfield Park, London NW5 1ER.

National Autistic Society, 276 Willesden Lane, London NW2 5RB.

National Childcare Campaign, Wesley House, 70 Great Queen Street, London WC2B 5AX.

National Childminding Association, 8 Masons Hill, Bromley, Kent BR2 9EY.

National Confederation of Parent-Teacher Associations, J A Jones (General Secretary), 43 Stonebridge Road, Northfleet, Gravesend, Kent DA11 9DS.

National Council for Special Education, General Secretary, 1 Wood Street, Stratford-upon-Avon, Warwickshire CV37 6JE.

National Council for Voluntary Child Care Associations, 8 Wakley Street, London EC1V 7QE.

National Eczema Society, Tavistock House North, Tavistock Square, London WC1H 9SR.

National Education Association, Ms M Smith (Secretary), 1 Hinchley Way, Hinchley Wood, Esher, Surrey KT10 0BD.

National Toy Libraries Association, 68 Churchway, London NW1 1LT. Information, training events, discounts and a magazine.

One-Parent Families, 255 Kentish Town Road, London NW5 2LX. Provides free confidential help on housing, law, day-care and employment.

Organisation for Parents Under Stress (also known as Parents Anonymous) 6–9 Manor Gardens, London N7.

Parents Anonymous (see Organisation for Parents Under Stress).

Partially Sighted Society, 206 Great Portland Street, London W1N 6AA.

Pre-School Playgroup Association,
Mrs Daphnie Knight (National Adviser),
10 Woodhaw, Egham, Surrey TW20 9AP.

Royal Association for Disablement and
Rehabilitation (RADAR), 25 Mortimer
Street, London W1N 8AB.

Royal National Institute for the Blind,
224 Great Portland Street, London
W1N 6AA.

Royal Society for Mentally Handicapped
Children and Adults (MENCAP), 117–123
Golden Lane, London EC1Y 0RT.

Scottish Council for Spastics, Rheumore,
22 Corstorphine Road, Edinburgh
EH12 6HP.

Scottish Parent-Teacher Council, Atholl
House, 2 Canning Street, Edinburgh
EH3 8EG.

The Spastics Society, 12 Park Crescent,
London W1N 4EQ.